*the celestial voice of*

# DIANA

# *the celestial voice of*
# DIANA

## her spiritual guidance to finding love

*channelled by*
**Rita Eide**

FINDHORN
*Press*

Published under license from
Hilt & Hansteen Gruppen, Oslo, Norway.

First published in English in 1999


ISBN 1 899171 03 7

Edited by Tony Mitton
Layout and cover design by Thierry Bogliolo
'Lady Diana Cosmogramme' © Marko Pogacnik 1999


Printed and bound by WSOY, Finland


Published by

## Findhorn Press

| | |
|---|---|
| The Park, Findhorn, | P. O. Box 13939 |
| Forres IV36 3TY | Tallahassee |
| Scotland, UK | Florida 32317-3939, USA |
| Tel 01309 690582 | Tel (850) 893 2920 |
| Fax 01309 690036 | Fax (850) 893 3442 |

e-mail info@findhornpress.com
http://www.findhornpress.com

# Table of Contents

The 'Lady Diana Cosmogramme'                                    6

Foreword to the Findhorn Press Edition                          7

Preface
How the Diana connection started                               11

Introduction
The initial channelled speech that Diana
gave in public on September 10th, 1997                          15

Part 1
Changing Perspective                                           19

Part 2
Higher Education                                               83

Part 3
Personal and Global Responsibility                            115

## *The 'Lady Diana Cosmogramme'*

The 'cosmogramme' above was designed specially for this book by Slovenian artist and author Marko Pogacnik. In Marko's words, "This is the sign that I see above Diana's head. It is moving all the time in–out like a kind of breathing."

Marko Pogacnik is the author of three Findhorn Press books:
- Nature Spirits & Elemental Beings: Working with the Intelligence in Nature *(1997)*
- Healing the Heart of the Earth : Restoring the Subtle Levels of Life *(1998)*
- Living Earth and the Presence of the Christ: A Fifth Gospel *(to be published in the second half of 1999)*

# Foreword to the Findhorn Press Edition

Were you one of those, who, in the days after Princess Diana's death, found yourself moving into a sense of greater connectivity as you witnessed and shared in the outpouring of grief? It seemed then as if the whole nation of Britain and much of the world beyond had been propelled into a new dimension where greater awareness and sensibility were normal; unusual, because this feeling was both intensely individual and widely shared. And amid the grief there was this awakening sense that we were not alone, our grief was shared, and in this support there was even a little joy, because our life grew stronger in the face of death. When the reader begins this very personal book, he or she may well find themselves returning to that same complex of feelings.

If these feelings were to have a name, they could be called 'heart consciousness': thinking along the planes of feeling, where love, relationships and connections guide reason and logic, rather than the latter being a law unto themselves. The book describes the 'conscious heart and higher mind' as an engine for responsibility and empowerment; as opposed to ego consciousness and sub-conscious programming, which is a recipe for irresponsibility and victimisation.

Is Diana really the author of this book? A moment's reflection will indicate why she should be. It is heart consciousness that can guide us in the amazing new world where we are travelling at such astonishing speed, where religious fanaticism, pollution, disease and population pressures confront the potential for information, technology, and abundance. Whether one's viewpoint is material or spiritual, this is a new evolutionary step for Mankind. The book continues in a vaster context the style which the Princess Diana was beginning to demonstrate on earth. And instead of observing her actions in heart consciousness, the reader is invited to participate with her, amplifying her impact a thousand or a hundred thousand times . Diana makes plain that she wants us to do this, and promises to be present with the reader.

The first part of the book explains the many changes of perspective which follow death, ranging from specific subjects of earthly interest, such as crib death, to the exhilarating freedom which comes with stripping off her "clothing of limited personal thoughts, the illusions of the conditional mind..." The second part of the book describes the 'Higher Education' which we are all about to undertake in order to move into our next phase of evolution. The last part speaks of our personal responsibility to make this happen. Heaven is not all bliss. Diana speaks of the sadness of her physical separation from her sons though she is present with them always. But she is quite clear that this book is not the place for family business.

In itself, the book is a delightful read. Being English, I felt as if I was taking tea with an elegant and charming hostess, engaging in a wide-ranging conversation with one subject leading to another, seemingly random but always witty and interesting. Others may find themselves wherever they are comfortable and happy; walking in the woods, dancing in a club or bathing on the beach; and Diana will be there. It does not feel as if one is simply reading; rather, as if the rhythm and impact of her words, their very beat, penetrate past the brain and dance into the body's cells. And indeed, Diana tells us that the book is written on several levels to reach different parts of our consciousness. Some passages are difficult to comprehend. Diana's advice is to read them anyway. Presumably, we will understand them when our consciousness evolves as promised.

Considering its small volume, the book's range is enormous. Many of the concepts are familiar to readers of spiritual material: chakras and kundalini; echoes of Plato and Theosophy. Other concepts are less well-known: it is the attraction for the forbidden that ensures our evolution; the excitement of being in the third dimension, i.e., human, where every action leads to an unknown consequence; the lure of that excitement for fourth and even higher dimensional beings who can find that their reality of instant gratification becomes boring; and the bliss of simply being human, independent of achievement and behaviour.

As if in passing, the book affirms alien abductions, government cover-ups and corporate conspiracy involving the World Bank, all the while confronting more fundamental issues such as the guilt and fear which arise out of religious misconceptions, or describing the reality of the Cosmic Christ and exploring the concept of God in a multiplicity of universes. One has to ask oneself, is this Diana whom critics called under-educated? Or was she much brighter than she was given credit for? Or do we really learn and observe so much more within a few months of death? Though of course, one is outside time after death, so earthly months and years are irrelevant. Diana herself says that there was much, particularly of New Age material, that she wanted to read but could not make the time for; also, that her personality was suppressed and she was not allowed to shine.

This book is not a stand-alone recipe for consciousness shift and global harmony. It is part of a concerted effort by many beings, including some from our own dimension, to help the human race embark on our next evolutionary step and take our rightful place in the cosmic harmony. Many other books point us in the same direction, to take personal responsibility for our lives, control our thoughts, focus on love and forgiveness, and empower ourselves to take leadership roles. Yet this book has a penetrating impact and is empowering of itself. It is recommended for all readers who have the good of the human race at heart. And Diana, Queen of Hearts, will be with them, for she will not be silent.

Tony Mitton, Editor
Findhorn Press

 Preface

## *How the Diana Connection Started*

Perhaps you wonder how my adventure with Diana actually began? I will try to tell you about this initial connection in the next few pages.

For a start, you need to know that I have been a medium, a so-called conscious channel to higher consciousness, for over 5 years now. This means that I am quite accustomed to recognising the various entities by their appearance and energies within and around me, prior to channelling their messages. However, I usually channel higher dimensional entity groups or ascended masters, and was not actually accustomed to be a spokeswoman for recently departed human beings at all.

I do not leave my body while I channel, so what is being said has to pass through my own limited consciousness, and therefore may become a little coloured by my own personality, my own way with words. Understand that in order to channel this way at all, I have to surrender myself completely to the process. I have to let go of my own thoughts and opinions and become an objective listener.

When I deliver a channelling, it is as if 'I myself' have the sense of withdrawing into the back of my head, and just allowing the appointed energy being to come in and use the empty space. This means that I can hear the words as they come, but I do not think them although I voice them. They just pass by in a fast flowing stream. In fact, sometimes too fast to get all the words into place. I might add that one of the benefits I receive during a channelling session is that I get a wonderful feeling of oneness with the messenger, and thereby come to experience their love and consciousness as part of my own being. It is a very blissful state of being indeed, but also rather draining on my physical energy system.

I am writing this book based on vocal channelling from the spirit of Diana, which was spoken directly into a tape recorder. It has then been written down word by word, in the same order as it was originally given, with a few minor corrections inserted for clarification and to make it more readable. Each chapter marks the beginning and end of each of the channelling sessions. Here and there, in between, she has also given some additional text along the way.

Like everybody else, I had seen or read some of the stories that the mass media brought forth regarding Diana, the Princess of Wales, the unhappy princess who did get the prince and the glamour, but ended up in loneliness and betrayal, and finally divorce. However, I especially remember an interview she gave on television at the time of the separation. Among other things, she said, "she wanted to become a queen in peoples hearts." She also admitted to adultery as well as telling about her eating disorder, and this candid speech became a turning point in my understanding and feelings for her.

I suddenly recognised in her eyes the tremendous wisdom belonging to a very 'old' soul and the love in her heart became obvious. In that moment I also mirrored something about myself, and ever since, as I looked at pictures of her, I could not help but feel a familiarity that rather haunted me; as happened on the day previous to her death, when I was looking at photos of her in a magazine.

Suddenly, then and there, I felt a strange sensation in my body, as if I were looking at my own face and my own body in those pictures. A similar thing had actually happened a few times before, but to a lesser degree, during the previous months. Rather confused, I was inwardly asking my guides, "Why does this happen? Please tell me what is going on here?" I did not get an answer right at that moment, so I decided that, OK, I would be told in due time...

The very next morning as I was sitting down to have breakfast, they broke the news on the radio. Diana had died in a car crash early that morning. I was utterly shocked and then started to cry, like so many others. Why did this happen? I was especially upset because ever since that television interview, I really had high expectations of her further work. Her task seemed to include doing international charity work and bringing love and compassion into world-wide focus. I had recognised this ability in the eyes of her soul.

However, as the reports on the reactions to her death started to come into focus, I realised how she had chosen to do her work, and in my heart I thanked her and The Creator for this genius turn of events. But before that, the morning after her death, I had been sitting there, grieving the loss of her life, her beauty and gracious-ness, and the love she had just found, when all of a sudden I recog-nised her etheric presence in front of me.

She gently looked at me and smiled, and then she telepathi-cally transmitted the three words; "I love you." I was stunned for a moment and then broke into fresh tears. For in the twinkling of an eye I understood all the answers to my questions of the previous day. She was bringing the message from my own soul, our soul, for I believed she was a fragment from the same soul as myself. The message that is so difficult to hear within oneself is the message of love from The Creator to his children, which holds the promise of eternal love, through the eternal soul.

Here she stood so lovingly in front of me, when the whole world was praying for her soul after this tragic accident. She seemed so whole, so filled with her godliness, and the message most important for her to convey to the living was, and still is "I love you." For you are all loved this way from the spirit side, the eternal side of life.

She went on having a little conversation with me now and then in the following days, and it became obvious that she wanted me to channel her in public. I must say that at first I turned her down, feel-ing it was too preposterous, even within my own meditation group. But she managed to take me by surprise, and love, and the result is related to you in the next pages of this book, as Introduction to 'The Voice' of Diana.

After that event I felt content and thought that was it. I had given her message and I thought that she would perhaps become a household name in the channel community like other entities and masters who regularly bring their energies through the various mediums or channels world-wide. Then, a couple of weeks later, I happened to buy a channelled book on spiritual matters, dictated from a college professor who had passed away some years earlier.

As I started to read, I suddenly got Diana 'on the line' and she uttered the words; "I would like you to write my book – please?" The implications of her question absolutely threw me, but at the same time the playful energies she always brings with her became part of my thinking, and I promised to consider it. And so it all fell into place. A lot of the bits and pieces of what I knew about my mission on earth, or whatever it is I am to accomplish in this lifetime, became transparent and formed a wholeness for me to recognise.

And so here I am, within the attention and consciousness of you, the reader, passing on the message of love and eternal life in Diana's spirit, for the benefit of all. Enjoy, and open your mind to new concepts of ideas and ways of thinking which may become enlightenment – and this in turn will allow your heart to open up to your own divine life plan and the very meaning of your experiences in this life.

For aeons of time humans have asked these questions, and as always before, you are being told; "The answer lies within." However, the answer is not in your minds. No, it is in your hearts where you can begin to recognise The Creator as a part of yourself, and thus become once more one with the creation, through the act of surrender to your eternal soul.

For, like Diana, all that we know for certain is that at some point in time, some place in the near or far future, our time on earth will also run out. And then, the remaining questions will have to be answered; "Did I behave or act the way I really wanted to? Did I follow the direction of my heart, so that I can be content with my life – now that it is over? Or did some other part of me, my fear, my limited thoughts, my denials and lack of faith decide my words and actions?"

Remember, if you cannot answer, "Yes;" if fear so far has got the better of you, it is not too late. Your heart is waiting for you for as long as it takes. Holding eternal love.

Rita Eide, October 1997

# Introduction

## *The initial channelled speech that Diana gave in public on September 10th, 1997*

A very good evening to you ladies and gentlemen. This is indeed a very rare appearance, and I apologise for the fact that I am making this channel very nervous at this moment. However, it is my great pleasure and honour to be with you – as you are my sisters and brothers. This is not a well-prepared speech, but it is indeed a speech from my heart, from where I am now. And you recognise me, as I have known many of you in our previous lifetimes.

At this point you have been grieving my recent disappearance from earth. However, I want to come and tell you that you are to rejoice for the happiness and love that I feel here and now at this time and in this place.

Understand that indeed this has been a transmutation for me – a transition from a world which was, or is, in transformation, to a place which is what your world is going to become; just as you are now yourselves in a transition within your world, as is the planet earth itself.

You know my name, and you know my face. But most important, you know me by heart, except that you have not admitted to this fact yet. Indeed, you are on your own way to discover the master within, and in this process you will find that we have a lot in common. You will find your own princess, your own queen inside. For the queen of hearts is indeed the feminine energy, the goddess energy of earth and of the Mother Creator.

I am standing here along with my principals, my principals who are what you call the masters. The masters of love, who have been teaching me, disguised as they have been to my eyes.

Understand that within your heart, you are to discover this for yourself. You yourselves are the masters in disguise, you, your children, and your parents, all of you.

Understand that in the transition between the worlds, in-between the different dimensions, you are to travel on love, waves of love, waves of compassion, compassion for yourselves, compassion for each other. For you are all in disguise, you do not see who you are, for you do not listen to yourselves, your own hearts.

In the meantime, you see yourselves sometimes in the eyes of another, and in the deeds of another. The good deeds that you see and admire are deeds that you are to become yourselves. As you discover your own inner queen, so you act from the heart of this queen. For you are all the queens of all the hearts, and the princess of your dreams.

You have all been hiding this from yourselves, but you are now to start riding on this new wave of consciousness for the times to come. For I have left this legacy for you, a legacy that you all need to consider as being your own. And this is, "What can you do for earth, what can you do for the development of your higher qualities, of the inner energy of the feminine, the feminine part which is in harmony with the masculine?" For the inner prince and princess are to give birth to an inner child, the creative energy of the future, the energy that is the Christ Consciousness.

I have also been on earth many, many, years ago, a little more than 2000 years to be exact. Back then I was the mother of Mary, the Virgin Mary, and I gave birth to her with the love of all of you who supported me in the Essene community. We all knew of whom would come next, as that princess was born to give birth to the universal prince of Christ. Now as well, I want to give my gift to the world, as the midwife for the birth of the new global consciousness. So that you all can find it in your hearts to start giving of your own true legacy, the truth called love.

Give of your own gifts, the gifts that you have come to give, and the gift of love consciousness. The gifts of light, the gifts of unconditional love from the heart, the gifts of compassion, because this is what is going to lift the earth to a higher level of life energies.

Compassion is what got you down to earth in the first place, as you came to virgin Lemurian land, many, many tens of thousands of years ago. You had the gift of compassion for earth at that time, for the goddess soul which gave life to this 'new' planet, and you had the wish to develop the planet through the masculine part of your-selves, your thought.

Giving through the creation of the thought and mind, and the ability to birth new consciousness through the feminine, are again going to build the new era of love on earth. For this is promised.

And so it is that this upheaval that you have experienced in the last week or so after my departure has occasioned a rise of con-sciousness beyond your imagination, beyond your comprehension at this point. Because people have turned inside, they have turned to each other; they have discovered the act of compassion and the gift of love beyond sorrow.

Sorrow brought forth love, the love that has come to stay to give growth to this new consciousness. Not only for the people of England, but for the people of all nations, all countries. Because this is a global event, because you all have come with your own univer-sal knowing of love.

However, as you do not have the ability to see inside yourself as yet and to, let's say, treasure your gifts, at this point you will need to turn outside and mirror it in your surroundings.

Now, this was my little appearance to you. Do not wonder about this appearance, because, you see, I have a special bond to this channel as we are of the same soul and fragments of the same mother, the same essence. So I thank you for this meeting and we may even speak again later.

I love you dearly.

*Diana*

# Part 1

## *Changing Perspective*

I greet you, beloved reader. I will take this opportunity to invite you into my world as you invited me into yours, into your life, when you opened your heart for me, from the day I passed over until the funeral afterwards, as well as now in the present. Indeed I have grieved with you, in compassion for the sorrow, for your pain, as it was my pain you expressed through yourselves.

Not the physical pain involved in passing away, going into my present condition, but the pain of your own separation from your inner source. You all suffer from your supposed separation from the unconditional love, which I finally have returned to. However, that kind of love I didn't know then, just as most of you do not know it now, as it is not part of your daily awareness and routines.

This is why I have returned, because I truly want to share all this love with you and make you understand that physical death is just a dimensional shift into love. And at the same time I wish to give you hope for the future. For the future is now, the future is what you are building from this moment on. The future is your present actions that will be returned for you to react to. The future is the reactions to your actions taken in the here and now.

It is indeed a great pleasure for me to be taking up my task as a teacher from the spiritual realms. I always knew it was in my heart to share my thoughts and my values with some of the 'children' on earth. And I started out in my youth, you know, by working in a kindergarten.

However, this work that I am now given is indeed much more fulfilling because I can see how the fruits of my work are being extended to so many souls at the same time. Then later, you will perhaps be passing on your new understanding in turn to your own children, and thereby my work will be done on a much greater scale than I could ever have anticipated. And I also enjoy the opportunity of being able to speak my truth, speak in human words with the voice of my heart.

For this book will be an experience of love flowing between us, a book from my spirit to your spirit, as we are not apart – but the realisation of oneness is for you to discover. The truth is not 'out there'. To find the truth you just need to look within, into your own heart. The God-given gift that you are to give yourself is the redis- covery of who you are in the essence of your true being.

Since I am now sent to you from the light of God, you are becoming the receivers of the light of God, who is The Overall Creator. I am also at the same time at the receiving end, as I am receiving and sending my light forward as a channel to earth.

Like you, I was already having some light in and around me as I walked amongst you on earth. You could sometimes see that light coming from my eyes, and sometimes you could feel it pouring from my heart as well, when I was in the position to give of myself, which certainly I was not always able to do.

This is also my opportunity to tell you that I am still not an icon or some sort of a saint. I am indeed what you are all going to become, as you grow in your spiritual knowledge.

You see, although if most of the time I was feeling my inner pain and loneliness, I worked it out by extending love, and that love was given back to me in return, by your adoration. To express love may also be the way that you are coping with your inner pain. But sometimes love becomes distorted and we end up expressing it as anger, as words of hatred or bitterness and regret when we become self-centred. And all these emotions you normally condemn in yourself, and I condemned them in me.

The ability to transform all those emotions through love, and as love, was inside me, as it is inside you. This ability to express your true nature, which is love, is now yours. To honour your feelings is necessary. They should not be suppressed as has been done in soci- ety. The workings of society tell you that it is not done to show your feelings in public. And this has brought upon you a lot of sorrow, a lot of suppressed pain, as I know from my own experience. Self control at any cost.

I personally coped through my private pain by using food as a substitute. I was purging myself for feelings using food as a means, until I finally got help to understand that I needed to bring up my feelings, and not the food. I can look at this with great joy now, because it finally gave me the possibility of understanding my needs and doing something about it later on.

As I understood how to open up and take responsibility for how I felt, I started to honour all my feelings and finally became honest with myself and with others. And this is something I wish to convey to you as well.

As a matter of fact, you are all beings of different genes and inheritance when it comes to your outer expression. You all have different abilities to express yourself through intelligence and emotions, and varying ability to use language, let's say, with brilliance. But the point is not to become brilliant intellectually. The point is to be able to express love brilliantly, and you all have the same talent to do this, to open the door to your heart and express the same energy of love from The Creator, to become a unique individual vehicle of His/Her expression.

For you are all travelling along the ray of love. However, you have hidden from yourself that you are the love that you are seeking, and therefore you are confused and lost, and thus unable to travel back home at this stage. But, in the twinkling of an eye you can start to see the inside and discover this love for yourself. You just need to choose yourself once again.

You need to choose amongst yourselves as well. To choose each other as your companions; to choose the society you want to live in; and finally to choose to have the global connection from which you have separated yourselves through the many frontiers of the different nations

Instead of seeing your own country as a national treasure, with its borders separating you and making you different from other people and other countries, you need to open up these borders and become as acquainted with your outside neighbours as you are with the different aspects of your self. But this time, please look at all that you have in common, the likeness in your hearts, and stop being afraid of each other because of differences in appearance or behaviour.

This is what the next decades will bring about, as several changes on earth will take place, which in turn will cause a global change. This is what is prophesied as the end of the old times, the old ways of handling your affairs. This is what is commencing already, and it will develop towards the main turnaround in year 2012, or 2011 to 2013, around there.

It is not my task at this point to get into details about this major turn of events, but some of it will be revealed in later talks that I will give on behalf of our spiritual teachers. Understand that here in the realms of light I am surrounded by a group of highly evolved spiritual entities who are here in the interest of bringing education to the world, and updating the information from the spiritual to the physical dimension. I have been appointed to bring through some of this information, through myself and through my channel as myself.

 Chapter 2

I once again want to let you know how delighted I am to be able to communicate with you and truly speak from my heart. How beautiful it is to express the truth beyond illusion of thought.

Actually, I am aware of the fact that I have been known to have been recording tapes before, and thereby making the headlines*. But I was rather limited by my own lack of knowledge at that time. And I was not able to come forward as myself in order to speak out. This of course was because I rather needed to be covered up, in disguise, since I was not allowed to have my own public opinion, living a very secluded and conservative existence indeed.

Now, this is actually also a picture of your own lives, how you are suppressed by the society you live in, how your hearts have been forced into silence and your own opinions put down, in order not to disturb and make ripples on the surface. For aren't you all made to conform to the boundaries of society, by those people in power who are making decisions at the top, as I was by the royal family?

After the separation I became the outsider, a black sheep so to speak, having the guts to open my heart, while others were b(r)ought into silence. For there are forces behind the scene that do not want the truth to be known or spoken. That indeed is why I could never go on with my physical life on earth at this time, and get the kind of future that I wanted and needed for myself, not to speak of love life...

The agenda and the design of how my life was to come to an end was, however made on the spiritual plane. It was decided by the higher entities of both myself and the others involved, and thereby a higher part of the overall divine plan was put into action.

_____

* Reference to Andrew Morton's *Diana: Her True Story* (1992)

And it all came together and it will be shown to you through your own stories – history. Know that there are no accidents, whatsoever.

Because we are all part of that grand design of divine intelligence, and you have your own part to play on earth as I had mine. I am now part of an even greater design, a plan involving this whole universe, and I am indeed grateful for the opportunity to go into the higher realms and get on with a higher level of my educational path. You are all stepping up, as you step forward into the opening up of your own closed minds and hearts.

Understand that what you will see on earth in the next decades is indeed a change of perception, a change of heart and matter, a change of understanding, and thus every so often there will be unexpected changes in your own lives, as well as in the immediate surroundings.

There are for instance many, many voices that want to be heard through the individuals who are channelling these higher intelligences or entities, as the time has come to open ourselves up for the inner communication channel. This ability will be available, not only for the very few, but for an increasing number of humans on earth. As you open your hearts, you also open up the natural ability to speak directly from your souls.

I myself am part of the same soul as the one belonging to my channel, and that explains how we are becoming one as I speak. And, just as I am in training, so is she, and so we are part of the project that our soul has put forth in order to progress in our growth and understanding.

This is also the case with all of you. For you see, these are the times that will show you clearly that you need to take responsibility for your own lives, so that you stop going on like living dead, asleep and walking in your sleep.

It is the time to wake up to a greater reality than earth self-centredness, wake up to the greater love and understanding of the whole cosmos and universe. See that it is time to act upon your heart's desire, to follow your visions and dreams, instead of being ruled and controlled by fear, which for ages and ages has been your way of escaping your inner wisdom and truth.

Many are with me here, as I transmit to you. You probably can understand that I am part of this larger unit of souls who have gathered together in order to draw forth the understanding and the experience of unity on earth.

Know that there are also aliens and extraterrestrials from far around the universe encircling your planet at this time. Because you are all part of a larger scale of evolution, and therefore you are gathering together the fragments from different areas and different levels so that oneness will once again be the first and foremost energy on earth, the energy of unity with God, the One Infinite Creator.

You may know the energy by many names, but on the highest level the Christ Consciousness is the engine or creator behind this energy. As I am presently being propelled ahead in my evolution, the Universal Christ Consciousness is touching you as well while you are reading, or listening to the spaces between my words. For it is all encoded into the cells of your body, in your DNA.

This energy is a potential frequency that you have encoded into your physical self because you wanted to be woken up in time to get the message; for instance, to read these pages and thereby bring forth a new level of pulsating light in your own bodies. This process is called 'raising your vibrations'.

Actually, your body is not permanent or solid at all, it is flashing on and off all the time, at a very high frequency rate, always interchanging between waves and particles, just as quantum physics has detected. What you do not yet see is that this means that you are constantly interacting with the spiritual or etheric world to fuel your body with light.

The raising of your consciousness or frequencies is part of the so called 'light work' on the planet, in which you are all unknowingly participants. And by being in the light, you have finally to realise that you are also this light itself. You are simply divine, made out of the light, so to speak.

As you begin this realisation of 'Godchild' in yourselves, you start looking upon your neighbours and your fellow human beings with fresh eyes, and also start seeing your common foundation, the very earth that you are walking upon.

We are all somehow partakers of the earth experience, and we are all children of the mother creator that you reside upon. By being within the gravity of this energy that this female being exerts upon you, you are the children of 'mother earth' and the children of 'father heaven' at the same time, merging between the masculine and feminine poles of thought and matter.

You are indeed the fruit of the love of the universe, of the One that has made the human from its own blueprint. Because you are indeed a whole universe within yourselves. Each and every one of you mirrors it holographically in your cells and organs and through-out your bodies, in which you are the master creator. You are all a replica of the creator force itself.

Much of what has been hidden from you for many centuries will soon come to the surface, as the old energy needs to let go of its controlling grip on earth. Then understanding that is hidden deep within your own minds will surface. As you know, average human beings today are only using 10% of their brain capacity.

The understanding that, by using your intuition, you are all able to get through to your subconscious will open up to the hid-den parts of your own experience all that you have suppressed, and finally direct you towards manifesting what you really want in your own lives.

# Chapter 3

After my parting, much information has come through the media and books, and through journalists who are making themselves experts on my life, seen from the outside. In this regard, I need to say that to truly see my life and me, you need to look either from beyond, or from within. And in my eyes, many of the things that are being published are just subjective speculations.

Remember that truth is relative to all the people that are involved, so that a situation has as many facets of 'the truth' as it has participants to the story that is being told. It is easy to forget this as you read the print.

What is true or not true in my own case will come forth when the time is due... But as you know, it was not necessarily the story that I really had to tell that was most interesting to the press or publishers. Basically, they just wanted to publish scandals and make the tabloid headlines in order to make sensational news, rather than spread my simple message of compassion, love, and service to the world.

In general, everyone who benefits by inflicting pain upon others gets to meet their own motives at some point, and thereby must acknowledge what they have created within the course of their own lives. But I am not to judge in any case, I am just here to remind you of yourselves.

However, there is truly a bright side to the stories as well. And from my heart I really want to thank the many of you for the generosity and the attention displayed in order to help further some of the projects that I was blessed to put my name to. Thanks to the media, some of these cases have now received a focus that otherwise would perhaps never have been achieved. And indeed, it is my great pleasure to be able to say thank you to each and every one of you who has contributed of yourselves, with your loving attention and your money.

Know that the love which you feel I displayed for the people and causes presented to me and which I got assigned to, is indeed the love that you have discovered for your selves, for the fellow human beings with whom you all are beginning to identify.

By opening your own hearts towards me, you also get in return an opening up of love for yourselves, so that we can work together on the project of giving compassion to the world, and to yourselves.

This is indeed very important, to have compassion and patience for yourself, as you are just in the early beginnings of discovering your inner universe. What you can do for yourself, you do indeed do for the whole, because you yourselves are living in parallel personal universes and are reacting to each other by energetic resonance.

By the way, when you look at me, please do understand that my own motives were not altogether 'pure' at the time I lived amongst you. I needed the charity and the fundraising causes for myself as well, in order to be able to forget my own inner pain. And to be able to reach out when I was not able to reach in.

So please see me as a part of yourselves that was growing and learning, and now is in a position to go beyond and within. Thereby I can love what I see in all aspects of myself, my shortcomings too, also my needs, my denial and my ill tempered behaviour, which was not always noble, but oh so human....

I did finally start learning to become true to myself and to my needs as I saw then them. And now indeed I can enjoy the totality of what my life has been, and who I am, from a larger perspective of understanding. And this is also how you will be meeting up with yourself after death, or after the dimensional transition.

One of the main questions you will be presented with afterwards is going to be this big one; "What have you done in order to help others?" This is the question you will need to ask yourselves as you are passing over, and it is at that point that I wish that all of you were going to have the answer that you would like to be giving yourself.

It is my contribution at this point to remind you of the possibility which you have every day to be able to contribute to your fellow human beings with kindness and openness, thereby reaching out and giving where you have abundance.

Abundance can be many, many things, and it is certainly not necessary to become poor yourselves, to give away everything down to 'the clothes off your bodies', in order to display true compassion. No, understand that in order to be humanitarian, you don't have to sacrifice everything and become beggars yourselves. You are only asked to give from your abundance, to share it. And with love in your heart, abundance is a natural part of your life and your being.

# Chapter 4

I would like to clarify some issues regarding relationships. Although not being an expert in this matter as Diana on earth, I do now have the overhead perspective, so to speak. And this is why I want to come forward to tell you that every relationship you have with someone else is in fact a relationship with yourself; disagreements display a part of yourself that is not clarified within the conscious you.

Ultimately, all of you have only one relationship to clear and that is the relationship with your self. That is the issue of self-healing. The healing of the inner loneliness of dimensional separation, which contains the painful thought which says that you don't have a personal relationship with God.

In every relationship you see your own relationship with God. It is that thought of being separated and alone in the world that produces the feelings of loneliness and separation in your lives.

To understand relationships you need to see that you always mirror yourself in some aspect of another person. You are yourself sending out what you need to be met with in return. So what you believe of yourself, you will meet in the belief of another. And the love that you give yourself, or the denial of love, will meet you in the encounter with another.

You are involved in a constant dance of energies, in the sense that the thoughts and feelings which you yourself are sending out, and those which the other person is sending out, make up the emotions of the relationship that you get to return to each other.

This, of course, does mean that it is indeed a difficult task to keep a relationship clear of, let's say, emotional strain, because you have to clean out whatever has been bottled up inside yourself. And so has blocked you from feeling the stream of love that is available from the universal you; loving energy which sweeps in and around you at all times, except that you are unable to receive it unless you keep your heart open and allow your own feelings to flow.

Everything that you keep a lid on will need to surface and confront you, and if you cannot accept it in yourself, it will come to you by means of another who acts it out for you as your mirror.

For instance, it often comes back to you by means of your children, because children are especially sensitive and they easily pick up your subconscious signals, as do your partner, your parents, friends or work colleagues.

The signals are all there in the emotions you are holding onto regarding yourself: the thoughts, the feelings, your image, they all carry the signals that you are sending out for others to pick up and return to show you 'you' until you finally understand your self.

So in order to make a perfect relationship work, a relationship that shows you your own love for yourself, you must really have this love for yourself, because it can only be returned if you already have it to send out. Which means that you cannot expect another to give you what you deny for yourself.

Most of you are doing exactly this, however. Indeed, you want your partner to give you the love that you are lacking in yourself. And so there is a constant lack of love in these relationships, either from one side or the other and at various times.

This cannot work; this has to lead you to personal disaster. And what you see going on at this point in time is in fact a rapid change of partners, all for the sake of learning about yourselves. The various parts of broken-up families are then in turn making new beginnings, most likely in other hopefully different and better relationships, for the benefit of all I might add.

Truthfully, you have got to work with your own denial of love, and this has to be mirrored. So be aware what you are asking for when you pray not to be alone, when you want to get a partner. Because he or she may not seem to be the person of your dreams, because they will act as a mirror placed in front of you so you can see your own denials and start to heal your self.

To heal your self is to let in the spirit of the Creator Force that created you in the first place, your spirit, your body, and your mind, your emotions and your feelings.

Know that in my earthly relationships I did not know what I

was looking for at the time, and I did not know what to expect either, since this was not a conscious part of myself at that time.

But I had this ongoing dream of being loved, a love which I felt I was losing or being denied when I became separated from mother through the divorce of my parents. And as it turned out, it was physical and emotional comfort I was constantly seeking. I could not find it in myself as I had disconnected from my true self in order to become the public figure of The Royal Princess.

I actually thought that I had found what I wanted when I got married to Charles and thereby was secured within the royal wedding locks. However, even this particular golden cage did not remain closed for long, as you well know.

Even in such a restricted marriage, it had to come to a break-up, because I simply could not live with myself, so to speak. I could not go on living with Charles because he mirrored a part of myself – my own denials – which I was not able to understand, nor did he. We were both seeking each other out in order to repeat a childhood disappointment.

Basically, he did not really want me as he was all of the time looking for an unavailable mother, found in Camilla. This third person was our way of escaping from our selves. She mirrored back to us the denial of the whole relationship and the foundation that it was built upon.

But bear in mind that this whole thing was not a failure as I see it from this perspective. Indeed it had to come to a conclusion, because we needed to force ourselves to go on with our lives, searching for what we did not have but were hoping to find.

Later, as I met others, there was still a need for me to keep on seeking for the perfect man in my life. And as I started to think I had found the ultimate love, the ultimate was indeed catching up with me, and it physically ended before it really began.

You see, I was not really ready to love myself as Dodi told me he loved me. And he was not ready to receive the love that I felt for him either, other than on this present plane of existence. For we were each other's soul twin. And that kind of love is 'eternally yours'. So in our higher minds and hearts we chose to do the transition together, in order to heal the wounded relationship part of ourselves, and thus finally join together in the next level of our existence.

Indeed, we are resting in each other's arms ever so often, to put it that way. But this doesn't mean that it continues in the sense of relationship terms as it was on the physical plane. Here we do not have the possibility, or the need, for a physical body contact in the terms that you understand contact.

Here we merge in our hearts, our essence, but there is not a physical kind of merging. However, our love itself is merged and this is utterly fulfilling, if I may say so.

However, many of you, although still in your physical existence, are heading for a relationship breakthrough. Because the consequence of your ongoing personal development is such that you may be meeting a higher and more developed part of your own twin soul as you go along. In this way you can meet up with the part of yourself that is able to do the healing from inside. And therefore the two of you will meet, to heal yourselves through your relationship with each other.

This may not always be a dance on a bed of roses; it does have its ups and downs where you may get pricked by a thorn as in all other relationships. But the rewards of love are also going to be much more fulfilling, because you become able to merge on all levels, physical, emotional, intellectual and spiritual.

For as you merge with those higher parts of yourselves inside your being, as well as with your physical partner, there is a profound feeling of love appearing; a love energy that is able to penetrate throughout your bodies, through your emotional feelings and through your minds, a sensation that will take you to greater and greater heights of exultation.

You will be introduced to a divine state of ecstasy as you merge together and get your bodily satisfaction, an orgasm that will give you glimpses of emotional ecstasy that you would not believe possible unless you had experienced it yourself. This is feasible when you open for your true love through lovemaking, when you are having sex made with divine love.

Sex, the physical part of love, is indeed meant to be a way of joining the love in your heart in such a manner that, through the act of lovemaking, you get in contact with the love of your own heart. And thereby you can start expanding the natural ability to receive and give love throughout and within yourself.

Sex is meant to be enjoyable; sex is there for the taking and giving. Not just in the sense of using each other for your own benefit, but indeed to share of yourselves, share your bodies, your mind, your emotions, and thereby merge your souls.

This is what sex is given you to do in all aspects of your selves. You share your sex with the opposite, to feel both the masculine and feminine part of yourselves in one body at the same time. The man can feel the female absorbing him, and the female can feel the man filling the empty space within. This is the ultimate merge that will make you into one essence when the dimension called time will be expanding, and you will become able to go beyond the illusion of physical separation.

This experience of oneness gives you also the ability to use the intelligence of the higher mind through the will of the heart, and thus is a way of spiritual development which is not given to you unless you are able to handle the consequences.

For the consequences are obvious: the impact of a high-energy power within you, a power which can heal instantly and a power which can destroy. That is why it is essential that you should be able to steer this energy by the willpower of the heart, with love; and not by the will of some lower part of yourself, your ego, which is motivated by fear.

This is what humanity will progress towards, as you develop love within yourselves. Because love is the doorway to the higher mind, but you cannot merge to oneness and open the door to the higher mind until you have learned to use your energies with love.

For those who prefer their own sex, one way or the other, that is perfectly OK. Homosexuality is just a past life leftover, as the person finds him – or herself trapped in a body of the opposite sex, but with the same gender feeling as last time around. You all get to experience this, in one life or another. It is just another way of balancing unfinished business towards oneself. And if you don't have a partner at all, you do always have yourself.

By the way, sex is not the only key to open this door, there is always meditation. But lovemaking happens to be the method I have chosen to focus upon at this point.

I will also speak to you about the issues around children that are aborted in the womb, at the beginning of their physical existence, and children who die just after birth.

I know that the issue of abortion is a great burden for many of you, because of the moral issue you feel is involved in choosing that life should continue or be extinguished by your own will, or even for your own personal comfort.

From a spiritual perspective you should know that souls come into physical existence by applying the process of merging positive and negative polarities, or opposite genders. It is an act of love-making between spirit and biological matter, higher and lower consciousness. The spirit superimposes its specific code of light upon the commencing biological life process.

It happens the same way in the act of fertilisation in the laboratory for test tube babies. It remains a sacred event, of merging spiritual light from the soul with physical matter. And it is indeed the birth of human conscious life in any case, whether it is inside or outside the bodies. However the spirit is only overseeing the growth process of the foetus during the pregnancy and it does not normally incarnate itself into the flesh until just before or after the time of physical birth.

Those spirits who come into the flesh just to spend a short period of time in the womb or following birth are in fact often higher dimensional angels who are stepping down their energies in order to offer their help in the physical dimension, or astral dimensions.

In this process they are able to step down their previous life form energies in order to get new work assignments as guardian angels to their parents, or they can go elsewhere as they are needed.

When a foetus is aborted either by choice of its mother or by choice of itself, it does not in any way mean that this life is lost. On the contrary, this life has come to a beginning and an end and a new beginning, and thus it is able to do its work wherever it is directed. This means that it has been able to transform itself through the act of coming and going, in order to at all times contribute of itself where it is most needed. And quite often it returns to the same mother through another pregnancy...

There is always a new beginning to an end, for no body ceases to exist, it only changes its form. In any case, it does not mean that a woman needs to feel any guilt, or should feel that she is doing anything against the will of God, or against the will of the soul that is occupying the foetus. It is indeed an act of co-operation that is being managed on higher levels of existence.

Where the subject of crib death is concerned, you do not understand this phenomenon at all at this point. You are trying to look for the reasons of death in the physical respiratory organs, in the heart or the brainwaves, instead of understanding and accepting that this is purely an act of, let's say, the spiritual willpower emanating from the spirit of the babies. (This is only possible during the first year or so because by then the spirit has to decide to fully incarnate and attach itself to the biological body.)

So you see, in crib death the spirit that is occupying this little child has decided to leave its life unused and return to the realms of angels or resting spirits. The reasons can be several, but often it does not find the conditions in which it finds itself satisfactory to its perceived life plan. For instance, certain outer circumstances could have changed from the previous agreement between it and the mother or father, and so it simply decides to retreat.

But, bear in mind that this is always done in higher agreement with the parents, and therefore in accordance with the life plans that remain left behind. Because, please understand that the sorrow and pain that arises from the situation will make the parents grow emotionally, and thereby realise deeper parts of themselves which would otherwise lie untouched.

These small bodies with great wise souls do indeed have the

abilities to touch hearts and give love, and even if it is not for long, it is still enough time to open the hearts of the family. In the pain of the loss, those who remain can start to open the channel of love within them.

They can start to make necessary changes in their lives and in their perceptions, and develop insight and evolve. And thereby they get a new perspective on life and of themselves. This spiritual reasoning goes for all kind of loss, especially those which happen when a loved one departs through physical death, whether they die young or old.

Unfortunately, this kind of personal growth happens mostly through personal pain, through loss. But this is because it has proven to be the way you learn the fastest, since you are not normally willing to be taught the lessons of growth given by the spirit, except when you are forced to listen.

When you live your life in the security of the known, in daily routines, you do not choose the unknown, because you feel afraid. It threatens your very foundations. But the workings of the soul are not ones of fear, but indeed of courage, and the soul honours all the steps that you take on your way.

Know that no step is ever wrong in the eyes of the soul. If you do not work out the situation in the first place, you will have new opportunities given to you.

Now then, this leads to the point, to the understanding, that you do not live only once as a human being on earth as you may suspect. You are recycling at regular intervals between the spiritual world and the physical life, and so you gain more and more experience of living and of coping every time you are on earth.

However, the lessons may be varied and thereby confusing, in the sense that you are perfecting yourself in certain areas but you do not see the whole picture and understand your whole being at one time, in one lifetime. That is, until you start to get in touch with your inner self, your soul, and the plans that are made on the higher levels of yourself.

But hey! This is the end of the nineties, this is the New Age, the age of the star sign Aquarius, the time which will force you to go within and heal your emotions, heal the split between mind and feeling, intelligence and the subconscious.

There will be a bridge between the subconscious and the higher mind which will enable you to take control of your life through your thoughts and feelings, and thereby get yourself into harmony. You will heal the denied parts of your own being. And this is only possible when love is present in all the chambers of your heart.

# Chapter 5

Let us take a good look around. What is going on in the world today? What is going on in the environmental area? What is going on with the very soil that you live on? How about the waters, the air, the vegetation, which are all becoming increasingly polluted, even as I speak?

It is all in turmoil, as you well know. As I speak, the phenomenon of El Niño is building up to breakout, and you may witness weather patterns you had never expected to see in your lifetime. Your world is simply changing.

This, by the way, is what the prophecies are all about. Now you have to own up to your own previous decisions. You have made decisions a long time ago regarding your own future on this planet. And although you say that you didn't know, the fact is that you have been told over and over again.

As it says in your Bible, "What you sow, so you will harvest;" what you give out, you will receive back. You have been living for today as if tomorrow never comes, and have not been willing to see the impact of your current actions. Understand that doomsday is every day in your own consciousness. Because you are demeaning yourself and your environment every minute that you live, by your own actions and the reactions to those actions.

What is catching up with you are your common decisions about what you should do in order to preserve what you have left. For instance, how to make food supplies last, and how to harvest what you have put into the soil. All over the world you harvest and sell to the highest bidder. Then you have thrown away what was left over in order to keep up prices, and now you have to pay, literally speaking.

You see, there will be a shortage of food, shortage of water, shortage of the very air you breathe, and it is all because of your own past lack of understanding, your refusal to listen.

But now, this is the time to react differently, to start acting in a new way. To start planning for the future by using your collective hearts, and not decide through your pocketbook of a mind, like unfeeling zombies.

You see, you are not zombies, you are human beings made out of flesh and blood and with a nervous system, which makes you responsible for what you feel and how you react to your feelings. And the inputs that your ego selves have loaded into your brains are no longer to be the master of this vehicle that is carrying you around in your three-dimensional lives.

Your consciousness, that which you are, the inner master, is living in the heart, not in the human brain.

By the way, your scientists are indeed just about to acknowledge that the brainwaves are monitored from the beating pulse of the heart, and that the two wave systems are always intercepted and ruled by feelings.

Because of your own collective mistake, you are used to thinking of yourselves as the masterminds, the rulers over all other life on earth. You are proud of your own brain which you think has developed over millions of years. The reptilian brain tissue has, certainly, but the newer part of the brain was added at a much later stage, not by mutation, but by outside intervention.

The fact is that you are not the only intelligent race in the universe. And you will be very surprised if you are not ready for the fact that relatives or ancestors from the outside worlds, the stars, some of which are outside your own sun system or galaxy, are coming to revisit you.

The aliens, humanoids, have regularly been coming back to see what they once seeded onto the planet earth, because they once experimented, using their gene technology on the DNA of the early species, Neanderthals, and thereby made them into the so-called human beings, Homo Sapiens. Their intervention represents the so-called missing link in the development of the human race.

Then celestial beings of light were sent off to the planet in order to teach the young children of earth and to seed love consciousness in the human race. When they first arrived they were enjoying a five dimensional earthly existence for many, many thousands of years until they got tempted to experience the concept of free will, the possibility of experiencing themselves as physical human beings in charge of their own destiny. In biblical terms you may also understand this event as the Fall, the switch from god-given spiritual innocence to human intelligence which built up an alter ego as identity.

You will have to understand that the aliens are at a totally different level of development. And some of them developed just through their brains, and not through their feelings. Which means that you will experience them as unfeeling little grey scientific robots. However, they will be mirroring yourselves, for instance in the way you treat those in your society whom you call mentally ill or retarded.

Because this is how you yourselves are treating people who experience the world differently. You see them as mentally disturbed or as some kind of under-developed people, and you, the masterminds, are allowed to control them.

The sensitives amongst you, you declare to be lunatics and crazy, and you give them pills so that they will not endanger your environment, and you keep them locked in institutions as prisoners of your own race. And then you do experiments on them, you tamper with their minds and with their very existence through chemicals and electrotherapy.

You are acting as if you were their masters, and you will finally understand the analogy of this because some of you will have the same experience with the outside 'master minds', coming from different worlds into your planetary existence. They may be intruding into your lives, checking up on you in order to control you and your present development as humanity. For the most part, they are 4th dimensional humanoids who are able to interact with the 3rd dimensional level where you are residing.

They do in fact take you into their spaceships, they do probe you with different instruments, and you think of them as inhuman. You call them evil and aliens, and you don't see the reference to yourselves, because you have denied your ability to look into your own hearts and thereby find the compassion you need to show to yourselves, to your own race, and to the sisters and brothers that are living amongst you.

However, the alien threat will bond the people of earth togeth-er as one race, and this will give you the opportunity to change, in fact to make a lot of changes towards love and compassion and oneness.

Then it will be time to open up to a new treatment and under-standing of those that you call mentally ill, psychotic, schizophrenic or mentally disturbed; along with all others who do not look or behave like the so-called 'normal human being'.

Now, this is the scenario that will meet you first, because you will need to create this in order to see yourselves. But all along, at the same time, there are also the loving extraterrestrial beings that once again are coming to teach you about love. They are originat-ing from worlds filled with love beyond your imagination and understanding. They represent a love that is based on total recall of the divine presence within every being, a love that respects human life and all life as equal.

These loving extraterrestrial beings will mostly be in your envi-ronment within the 5th or 6th dimensional atmosphere of earth. However they will not probe you with instruments. Instead, they are sending you high frequency rays of information which consists of intelligent loving light. This in turn will open you up, and there-fore enable them to talk to you through your hearts and higher minds in a higher state of emotional awareness, when you are ready.

This is not schizophrenic hallucination, this is made possible through telepathy, and is very, very real. Then you meet the higher parts of yourselves, the sisters and brothers who once again are seeding love consciousness onto earth by re-encoding your altered DNA. Then you will be meeting another part of yourselves through soul connection in an open heart to heart dialogue.

What I am speaking of is not science fiction; it is already going on and the top-secret military units and governments are all informed, but they are keeping it under the highest degree of secre-cy. However, it is time that you demand to know, especially the truth regarding their own motives...

Fear and love is somewhat going hand in hand within your own understanding; because fear is what your common society is all about. Your society is denying love because it is feeding on fear.

Fear of not being like everybody else, fear of being socially aban-
doned, fear of punishment if you move outside the limited behaviour which is how human life is normally accepted.

You will need to look twice and rediscover the spiritual side of
humanity, and take a good look at what values you have created
within your society, and what you have labelled dysfunctional.
Indeed the dysfunctional is very often the most creative and therefore real. It is necessary to rediscover yourself because the so-called
normal is 'stagnation within limits', and you need to go beyond to
see your unlimited nature.

When you have started to learn to love amongst yourselves, to
love the human race as one, you are ready to face the so-called outside threat as one unit, and thereby become strong as a unified
human race. Then in turn you will be able to understand and for-
give, and thus share your newly found wisdom with the alien visitors; those who are now coming back in order to collect what they
once had left to develop in their own likeness, but whom you will
meet with the surprise of love instead of fear.

Thereby you will teach them, by helping them to develop what
is under-developed in their over-developed minds and egos. For the
feelings of love, which they themselves have lost in their quest for
the sovereignty of intelligence, is what you need to give them in
return for your own existence.

Because you are their children, and as their evolving children
you need to teach them the latest truth, and thereby the circle will
close. Otherwise, you will end up like them, living in a world based
on high technology but empty of love.

Understand that the further development of the human race is
going to take place in connection with the races outside of what
you understand as humanity; those races that are termed
humanoid and therefore very foreign and very alien to you in their
appearance, their ways of communication and means of travelling.

You will soon need to develop new abilities, like reading energy patterns, so that you will be able to know the intention of others
by feeling their energy impact on you. This way you will have the
necessary protection, with the necessary ability to carry your own
safety with you wherever you go and in whatever circumstances you

find yourself.

Your protection against unwelcome intruders within your space is the love from the heart, and your security is compassion because nobody can destroy you, the light, for the speed of 'supra light' exceeds all darkness. Indeed you are eternal, your soul is eternal light, and by knowing this you can finally overcome the fear of death and the fear of physical destruction.

Dying is only a transition from one kind of frequency of body to another kind of frequency of the speed of light; or speed of matter made up from positive and negative light particles, photons in standing wave patterns, which in turn make up the structure of your biological bodies.

As I speak to you now, I am presently in a kind of higher body essence which is faster vibrating and not physical in the sense that you can touch it in such a way that the touch will leave a feeling of solid structure in your hands. However, it is of a substance that leaves an imprint on the environment in the sense of electromagnetic impulses, which you can also measure through my channel.

When she speaks on my behalf, you will notice a different heart frequency and different brainwaves from her usual state of being. This is because I have imposed my energy upon her energy system, so that it comes out as a different energy pattern as we mingle and become one.

I normally speak with a voice commencing from the brain structure within her mental body, through impulses of energy patterns which the physical brain then in turn translates into physical words. It is also possible to become one in the emotional body and let her experience my feelings. However, then she becomes so choked up that she is unable to speak.

Understand that you need to revise the limitations which you are used to when you view a person within the frame of just the physical body.

The understanding that there are several interconnected higher bodies will become more and more prevalent; also because there will be an increasing number of people who are able to see some of the different energy bodies and therefore are able to verify these things which I am telling you. And of course not only me, but also all the others who are coming forth to give you information at this time.

It is not these clairvoyant people who are crazy; indeed they are very normal in seeing what is there, instead of hiding it from yourselves in disbelief as most of you do. Because you do actually see it; you see it but within your own mind you don't believe or accept what you see. So you close down this part of your own perception and tell yourself that it is to be stored away under 'unnecessary information' or in 'fantasy files'.

Because this is indeed what you have been told when you were little children and open to see the things that your parents or caretakers had forgotten existed. And little children will indeed be your teachers in the future because they will be able to keep their original vision, able to keep their hearts open and not be so much imprinted by the limited beliefs of society.

Old, knowing souls are incarnating in increasing numbers, with their ability intact to stay within their own energy frequency and thereby able, for instance, to remember their past lives together with their life goals, their purpose for being on earth. So parents, please watch out for your children and start to take them seriously from the moment they are born.

They will also be able to tell you their higher truth which they can still remember from previous existences. And this will create demands for a new norm of teaching and a new norm of learning, and so the overall educational system will be changed as a result of this influence.

The wave of these Star Children contains many souls who are coming with their own wisdom, love and understanding, and also a refusal to negotiate in order to forget their own inner truth, as they are very strong-willed personalities. And they are already here as part of this wave of consciousness that is growing in your society. I should know. I was one of them myself.

These Star Children, these wise old souls who are termed Children of the Light, will also force their parents and authorities to change the way they are handling the issues of environmental protection, of government influence on private life and on business, and the issues of politics altogether.

This means that the economic system will merge with the ecological system, so that the very distribution of wealth, growth, food and merchandise will be distributed directly through the hands of the people, from person to person, by networking.

This is indeed a remarkable change. It has already started, and although governments are trying to keep a lid on it, this network-marketing will explode more and more and force itself through the national frontiers and overcome the restrictions and limitations that politics are trying to put upon it. Just take a look at what is already going on the Internet.

Now, it is not for me generally to be speaking like a politician, but, as clever politicians do, I am also jumping ahead of time to pick up what people want in order to be able to lead the way. Not however along the narrow pathways of your frightened minds, but instead on the joyful road of following your hearts.

If you see a political ambition in me, it could be that I do indeed intend to be a guardian of the growing heart wave that is to develop on earth. An ambassador that has come back as a messenger from beyond to give you the proof or understanding that you need, in order to go by the will of your own heart instead of being led by the outside authorities. You just wait and see, as you start to believe, the manifestation of miracles can begin...

Many of you were of the opinion that perhaps I was not very intelligent in my lifetime as Diana, because I seemed to give the impression of being rather preoccupied with the way I looked, how I dressed, with my general appearance. But instead of talking to people through words, I was to convey a message of inner feminine strength and beauty which was not aloof in itself but was yours to touch and to become touched. I tried to give the understanding that the qualities that I represented were meant to be passed on and shared with the world.

These are also your qualities, of each and every one of you, no matter what your looks, no matter what your IQ score or intelligence. What you have brought into the world is your unique self and the ability to share of yourself through an open heart with an open mind, and this is the understanding that will bring you all together again as one people.

You will start to see your common features instead of the differences, and you will finally understand that you are sharing a very sacred space together, which is the planet earth. It is indeed a jewel in space.

Many, many, will come from the outside worlds to watch you go through this shift in consciousness. Most of them will not interfere, because that is not the will of the universe. The will of the universe is that you, by your own free will, are going to show yourselves capable of rising from the Fall. Rise from the darkness of your minds into the light, from egocentric consciousness to the universal will of the one heart, to find the love that you all yearn to experience. You will pronounce it as finally coming home.

# Chapter 6

My dearest brothers and sisters on earth, the time has come to give you some comments on my own death experience. A couple of months have passed, and I am beginning to be able to see it from within without too many emotions. You see, initially I was totally in shock, but not for long, as I was graciously met with the all-encompassing love and light emanating from our own brother Sananda, the cosmic name of the man known as Jesus. Who also happened to be my grandson, the first born son of my daughter Mary, as I was also living amongst you at that time, in Israel around 2000 years ago.

I just sort of flew into the light, because this is how I have to describe it. At that particular moment, as the car crashed into the tunnel wall, I just continued on straight into the arms of the most wondrous light you can ever imagine. And standing in the middle of this light with his arms outstretched was Jesus the Christ who embodies the Christ Consciousness on earth. For he is indeed the Son as you have always been told, but so are you and so am I. He embodies Oneness, but he is also, at the same time, one of the many. He was trying to show you that he and the Father are one, and so are you.

However, you as human beings have forgotten your higher parts; the part of your self that is called the Higher Self, the soul-consciousness which is the Christ Self. And the Christ Selves are all equal to each other.

In the moment of the car accident, as I myself flew out of my body, I changed my very appearance. I changed my energy patterns, from being captured in a physical body to embodying the 'Christ Outfit'. Which has the form of two 3-sided pyramids interlocked into a three-dimensional Star of David formation, or what is called a Star Tetrahedron, which is the universal form of the light body.

This light formation is holding your consciousness in place in all of your different bodies. This energy body also holds the blueprint for all the different bodies that you possess, and that includes the physical part of yourself.

Understand that there are many dimensions to every thing and every body. Those dimensions are built up from an ever continuously expanding understanding and merging of consciousness. It embodies separation versus oneness. This is the easiest way of explaining it to you.

Let us look at your own soul consciousness in terms of seven dimensions. There are more, but in this model we will use the sacred number of seven as a good basis for understanding.

The first dimension contains the elements of your biological existence, just the elements. It is aware of itself just as it is.

In the second dimension you see things in black and white, but you see it only from the understanding of a beginning and an end to everything. You may compare it to a confused little ant crawling around on the drawing of a circle made on a large sheet of paper. All he is aware of is the paper he is crawling on.

In the third dimension you gain some perspective; you are able to place yourself in the middle of the circle, rise up above the paper and see the formation of the circle around your feet, and you have gained some view, some height to your understanding.

In the fourth dimension you find yourself floating within a circular sphere, a bubble which surrounds you with no beginning and no end, and there is the so called 'no time'. Meaning that time is happening around you all at the same time; it is not linear any more, the sphere itself has become the time.

In the fifth dimension you find your self centred in the middle of this bubble or sphere, and from the middle you see that you have conscious access to the information contained in the sphere that circles around you. Which represents experiences in time through the different lifetimes, all at once. Not one life leading to another, but in a non-linear fashion, so that you see the totality of who you are.

In the sixth dimension you are able to connect with the six other spheres that are interconnected with your own as one sphere linking into another, forming the first group soul aspect of seven as yourself. Now you start to be able to travel beyond your individual soul-understanding in order to identify and reconnect your self with others.

When you have merged your selves throughout the six, you move into the lining containing all seven spheres. This circle in turn contracts and turns inwards on itself and you become one with the light within which contains the seventh dimension of your first entity consciousness.

Then it starts all over again; you merge with each other in greater and greater numbers of soul groups, and at the same time, when you go within, there is only one.

Now then, as I flew through the dimensions, as I discarded my physical body, it seemed like I went straight through these experiences of understanding and met up with Sananda in the seventh dimension. This is however an unusual procedure. It is only possible with a special kind of care and treatment for the person involved. And I was provided with this special attention because this was part of the plan, because I had been etherically prepared for the time ahead.

Which means that there had been energy work done on my etheric bodies so that I would manage this transition with the help of my higher dimensional selves and the masters themselves. Because I was appointed to be brought straight into my inner state of divine wisdom without a resting and recuperative period, which is the usual procedure when one passes through death without a moment's notice.

However, this light experience happened outside of time and space, and on the way through the dimensions my grandmother and my father also greeted me, along with some others who came towards me. This happened somehow before I melted into the brilliant light that I have spoken about. They came towards me and opened their arms and welcomed me. And I was told that my time had come, but that I was to go on to a higher dimension yet.

But then I hesitated, and in the next twinkle of a moment I realised what was going on. And in agony I inwardly screamed that I had to go back, that I needed to go back and take care of my most beloved babies, my darling sons, who are indeed two very, very precious little boys to me.

Then I was told that it was not possible, that my injuries were too severe and I would need to leave the body and discard the present earthly life. However, I was actually able to return for a little while until the agony of my pain got too intense and I closed my eyes to the physical world, and willingly passed on.

As I travelled through the dimensions, I suddenly understood the principles of The Divine Universal Consciousness and I understood that I was part of that principle and part of that consciousness, and that it was towards this part of myself that I was to return.

When this is said, I also have to acknowledge the presence of my beloved partner Dodi, as well as Henri Paul, our driver, who were both appointed to go through with the plan along with me – and in this way are greatly honoured.

At one point the three of us were actually brought into a huge heavenly hall, a brilliantly lighted hall with some kind of platform or stage in front, and here the three of us were presented; sort of being welcomed back into the spirit world.

Then as I looked out on the people gathered, I understood that I knew every single one of them. It was indeed like coming home from a long journey. And I could see that many of them had also been on earth, some of them in what you would have to call famous incarnations, appearing as celebrities, but at this level it was all equality.

It was all the brothers and sisters and darling soul-mates from whom I had been separated and missed in my heart for so very long. And so we joined, and it was done in a fashion that is not quite possible to describe in physical terms. Because it was as if I was being greeted by the energy of all-encompassing love, and this love was being transmitted through every cell of my so-called body or being, so that I was being fused with energy, and this energy was indeed the energy of oneness.

This energy I integrated and kept inside as I went on to join the Ascended Masters, where I was to get further instructions for my afterlife and the work to come. You may understand this as the process of the sixth dimension, which I needed to experience as

I was to be welcomed into the seventh heaven or dimension.

This whole journey was actually like one long moment or one rapid movement, because I was already out of the time and space continuum. So my experience was indeed one of passing straight through from the dark tunnel and into the light, and it felt like a journey of joyous transformation.

At the same time, as I travelled through the dimensions I 'stripped off' my clothing of limited personal thoughts, the illusions of the conditional mind, and I understood all of a sudden everything that I had not been aware of, confined inside a physical body.

As for Dodi and Henri Paul, they were put straight into a celestial hospital bed in order to recover, while I got this special energy treatment as I mentioned before. However, as it was the request of my heart, a part of me was also able to go back and stay with my sons as they got through the initial period of shock and grief of being presented with my sudden departure.

Throughout this whole time that has passed, I have been able to follow them very closely. Sometimes I have gently touched them with love in such a way that they have been able to feel my continuous presence, for which I am eternally grateful. I hope that this will continue also as they grow, and that they will not close down their sensitivity to the eternal love from their physical mother.

I see in their future that others will come in and fill some of the needs which I felt that only I could fill, but a lot of care will be given so that they both will be able to go on with their lives.

Indeed, I also want to ask of you, the public, that you do not put too much pressure on them, so that they will also be able to live with a personal space around them. Which I was not granted, but which they now will have a better opportunity to demand for themselves.

However, it is understandable, seen from your past and present conditioning, that you want to follow the lives of my sons closely, just as you look to other so-called royals, people whom you put in a special function within your life or society.

The royals are however some kind of survivors from a past time when royal people were supposed to have blue blood in their veins. Versus other people who had only normal red blood cells, they seem pretty special. But you know that this is the 21st century, and it is time that you take another look at the whole system of royal functions.

Indeed, I wanted to change those functions from being above the people to becoming an example amongst the people, to be close to the people, and not separated and aloof. I wanted to be part of the people as part of a privileged group, in a position to give of myself, and thus I was receiving a lot of love – from the outer society. As it is however, the royals have become a hunted group who feel they need to go on complaining about their lack of privacy. This is their way of survival.

Bear in mind that you are all wearing a crown on your head. This is the crown of your own divinity, the Godhead, the understanding that you all are the sons and daughters of the mother/father queen and king. Start looking at yourself as your own role model instead of looking at others, whether they are royal, movie stars, fashion models, or other kind of celebrity in art, work and sports; or whatever kind of idol becomes a celebrity because they stand out from the crowd.

Instead, you can look at your self within yourself and find what you have in you that will make you stand out to yourself, not for the sake of the crowd, friends, family or neighbours, but for yourself. For in the course of idolising others, you have lost your respect for yourselves. You have placed your respect in others in whom you see qualities that you don't see in yourself, which you deny in yourself.

You are all part of an archetypal essence, of which, this time around, you have chosen just a few parts for yourself. Although you do possess them all, you yourself cannot play out all the different roles in the same lifetime. Otherwise you would be too confused, with multiple personalities interacting on a full time basis.

But when you start to rise in consciousness, to rise above the centre of your personal reality, you see that you yourself actually do have all the possibilities in the world. You have just chosen to focus on certain specific aspects of personal experience in this lifetime. And therefore you are all equal, but on different levels of understanding and experiencing.

Understand though, that in this lifetime you have collectively decided amongst yourselves to open up to a higher understanding, to a higher level of your being. And even if you think you do not want this change, it will be kind of forced upon you, in the sense that you will have to open your eyes and make your own choice when the possibilities are being presented to you.

Because you can go with the flow or you can decide to stand still and stagnate, falling back into your old habits and your own pain, instead of reaching out and welcoming the help that is being offered you on all levels at this time.

Many of the light workers, the star-born children sent from the extraterrestrial forces of light, are showing their true nature on earth at this time. They are starting to give you examples of the development which you seek in your own search for stardom, in the sense that you are re-entering into the star within yourself. Indeed this star is centred within your own heart, and its light is shining in your eyes.

This is the twinkling, flowing light within your own universal body, for this is the inner light that is responding to the light from the stars, the energy from all the stars that you see far out into the universe. It is your own Higher Selves, your own higher under-standing, that is pulsating and shining and giving you inspiration and information. Although you don't see the energy lines them-selves, the flow of divine energy or 'supra light' is being brought back down to you at all times.

Now, you may be one of those people who has felt my pres-ence at your side and wondered how this is possible. But you see, from the seventh heaven or dimension where I am now a resident, I am in a position to share my presence with many of you at the same time. And this in turn is because, from the seventh level of myself, I am part of the energy grid that is, let's say, building the col-lective energy system in the etheric atmosphere of this planet.

You all have your own higher selves placed at different posi-tions within this grid. And those positions were set through the time and place of your physical birth at the moment you decided to re-incarnate on earth. The explanation of this specific position is given in your astrological star chart as your personal birth chart.

Know that you have not chosen a random place wherein to put

your self; indeed, it also has a karmic connection with the time and place where you arrived and departed from earth in each previous lifetime. And these points of reference are making up patterns, along with the other lives lived by everybody else, all complete with the marks that you have put into the history of earth.

You will find all these geometrical patterns contained as information in 'the grid' as your true history, the so-called Akashic Records of earth. You also carry along a replica of your own previous energy patterns within your personal grid system – in your energy bodies or Auric Field.

The Akashic Records are in fact the records of this planetary grid and bear the imprints which you have made together as earth history has developed. And some of you will also be able to obtain access to this grid while you live on earth and start selecting and transferring this information, but you will be given a lot of responsibility as you receive it and print it out.

This is of course important. Those of you who are so-called light workers yourselves, you understand that responsibility comes with the territory; it comes with enlightenment and the developing work that you at all times are committing yourself to do.

At night-time, all the time you are physically asleep, you are being presented with contracts. These are contracts of agreement between you and your co-workers, between your earthly self and your celestial self, so that what you agree to one night cannot be changed by your day-time consciousness the next day, unless you go back in and make a formal change in your contract.

The contract is necessary of course because it is well known that you vacillate and change your mind constantly, and, having free will, you cannot really be trusted solely on the basis of an oral commitment.

Now, that was a digression. I wish to get back to discussing what is going on in the overall picture. In the different levels of existence, your being is just as much a part of reality as is your earthly life at this time. And the enjoyable part is that you yourself are the hands above the marionette – the puppet on strings in the hands of fate – to which you sometimes compare yourself.

Although you may feel that you are being 'played' in your life, they are in fact your own hands which are holding the sticks and all the time making you move. So you may say that you have free will, and you do have a free will, but also you have a higher, wiser part of yourself that is always giving you information by way of an inner feeling or knowing, which you also call intuition.

In other words, you can choose freely, but you will be reminded of your responsibility for your choices and their consequences. And you will be corrected by a 're-action' at one time or another – if you should decide to ignore your inner voice of love and wisdom and go on a trip into despair and confusion, fuelled by the fear coming from your lower self, the ego.

It is your free choice, but the light will be pulling you back sooner or later. Although it is always up to you, yourself, to go on and 'enjoy' suffering, experiencing it in the ego, be it your own or the collective's, for as long as you find pleasure in fear.

You may think that all these things which I am speaking of are weird, and the workings of a crazy woman, departed in one way or another... But please understand that this is not craziness; the craziness is going on in your world because you have closed down your inner vision, the vision that looks into your self.

You are seeing others as your own role models instead of giving yourself the opportunity to star in your own play and take the leading part there; instead of playing some subservient role in somebody else's play of life, where you are becoming a victim or a supporting actor in your own play.

Or perhaps you bring others into your play and direct their lives through your own will, by controlling them. However, this is not giving you the satisfaction you are seeking. What you are seeking on the inner level of your self is not control of others, but control of your own life and love in such a way that you don't need to seek your love and approval from others.

And ladies and 'gentle men', it doesn't help to give all of your love away in order to get love back. Because love has to start within, and only when you have it and keep it within yourself will the others reflect this level of love back to yourself.

Then, as you lovingly open your eyes, you will see the divine, The Mother-Father Creator, in every single one of your co-players on the stage of life.

Because you, humanity, have come together as one into this world, into this level of perception, and you are finally going to be living as well as leaving together, in oneness.

You are presently going through the transition which will change your inner and outer perception, change the way you look at yourselves and the world of possibilities, and in consequence you will grow up. You are the children of earth who are finally to be given the education that teaches them to become independent of their mother, to become free-spirited, courageous children of the stars.

You are no more to be born for the benefit of parents who have shut down their own dreams and are trying to force their own lost visions and hopes upon the next generation, their sons and daughters; instead of taking responsibility for, let's say, their own misjudgement of their inner workings, of their inner voice. Those who try to make their children do for them what they have not been able to do for themselves will be met with total rebellion.

Truly, this education is giving you the opportunity to evolve into responsible, mature beings. And as you become responsible to your own selves, you will come to understand that you have responsibility towards the world you are living in and towards the people that are here along with you. You are all part of the same consciousness, and have the same responsibility because you are one humanity.

From this part of existence, I can only say that I am finally at peace with myself. And as a peace worker I come back to you and beg you to look for the same peace within your self now. Do not wait until you go through a transition from which you can't go back, through the door that closes to the physical universe, so that you have to wait for another possibility of incarnation.

Because, if you keep on evolving and receiving the light that is coming from the stars, from the star ships and from your higher selves, you will possibly experience, some of you within this life-time, that you will be able to transfer through physical death without losing your body. You will resurrect, like your brother Jesus.

You are simply going to be shifting the composition of your

atoms and molecules through the speed of your photons, in such a manner that you will transform within the physical body. Consequently, you will also be able to return to the physical world through the same vehicle, which is only shape-shifting from one dimension to the next.

This is possible. There will be an opportunity for time travelling as well. You are all multidimensional beings. This is your future and it is already starting, commencing in the understanding of the here and now. Because the light evolution, the enlightenment, can come in the twinkling of an eye, if you look inwards and surrender your selves to the voice of your soul, to the path of your heart.

In doing this you need to be totally honest with your selves because the soul cannot tolerate dishonesty. Honesty is required within the body of your feelings and in the way you behave towards others and let others treat you, so that you can stay within your heart energy all the time and so keep the frequency of the higher dimensional soul self within your physical body.

Then the Inner Light will shine as a sparkling jewel within your own eyes. And in your auric field there will be a tremendous amount of power, and in your own hands too, in your own etheric and physical energy system. This means you will be able to heal the patterns of pain from the past and start living here and now in unity and in totality, which is the wholeness of being. As your beloved brother Jesus the Christ came to show you.

# Chapter 7

Now, I want you to take a good look at yourself. Just how do you look at yourself? Do you look at yourself in the mirror or do you sit down in a quiet place and look within. Listen within? Most of you run to the mirror, unless you feel you have enough subjective knowledge of yourself to look inside neutrally as if you are viewing the picture of another.

It is a fact that most of you tend to look at yourselves only from the outside, or superficially. Then these are my next questions: how do you value yourself, how do you value your life, how do you value who you are?

Most of you will answer by counting up all your past efforts, your education, your work, your achievements, your personality traits, the way you behave and so forth. However, none of you, or that is not normally, will sit down and value yourself for just being alive. But this is how the spirit part of yourself values you.

Value the precious gift of your life. Because if you had been able to value yourself just from your inner being, for being alive, you wouldn't need to worry about how to make yourself happy. For then happiness would be there all the time. Because the evaluation would be coming from the light within, the joy within, the very joy of being part of the wonderful creation of which you see but a small fragment when you have the physical limitations that you have placed yourself in.

Know that all of you are responsible for your own life and for the happenings in your life. You are responsible through your thoughts, through your feelings, through your intentions in every second of your days. As I have mentioned before, you are all the time creating the future by your actions in the here and now.

If you were able to sit down and evaluate yourself, not by your actions, by what you do, but instead start evaluating yourself just by being you, just by being able to have gotten a ticket to physical life in the third dimension, you would get a whole new perspective on your life.

Just being the lucky one out of the competing crowd that has been queuing up in line for so long in the fourth dimension or fifth dimension, or even sixth dimension, should be enough reason to celebrate. And just knowing that you were found worthy of a ticket to earth at this very important period in history should make you very proud of yourself indeed.

Because the lessons on earth are so many and so diverse that the beings in the other dimensions treasure the earthly adventure very highly. As you would perhaps have treasured a trip to the islands of Hawaii, let's say, or some other exotic place far away from your daily environment.

You see, although it may be hard to believe at this point, even life in the heavens can become boring in the long run. When you live in constant loving bliss in paradise, where you get to rest and play and just enjoy being in the constant 'sunlight', you finally get up your strength and start to feel like getting back to tough 'work' again. And hardly anywhere else is there so much unfinished business to be attended to as presently on planet earth....

You may be surprised to hear this, but you see – although what you experience on other planes of existence is the bliss of divine beings – it does not have the excitement of being physically alive, of experiencing the unknown. Of being able to create, create with every feeling, every motion of your own being – and not know the result until some time in the future...

This is a very precious gift, because you are moving by your own will and in that sense are free to recreate who you perceive yourself to be, in every aspect of yourself and every moment of your life.

For instance, on the astral level or fourth dimension, you instantly create everything you want, there and then. By using your thoughts, it will appear right away in the moment, just by thinking it. What fun! you might think, but for how long do you think that this will keep you amused and satisfy your craving for new adventures?

As it is, you do not yet value this gift of creating into the unknown on the physical plane. Because you seem to think of the universe, or of the future, or of the daily struggle, as some kind of punishment that you must endure before you can get out of your miserable life. And then you get depressed and even think of suicide instead of prolonging your efforts to be alive, changing your perception, and thereby creating the life that you really want for yourself. Depression is the sadness of the soul trying to tell you that you are not following the path of your heart.

Another thing you really need to understand is that the religions of the world, like Christianity, have much to do with your misconception of your lives. The thought that there is a vengeful god who is punishing and rewarding at every turn of events, depending on your deeds, depending on whether you are being good or bad according to his own set of preferences, was planted by humans seeking power.

This in turn makes you look at yourself always in terms of judgement, in terms of doing the right or wrong thing. While the truth is that there is no such thing as a father figure in the heavens who is judging you. There is only the overall creations, allowing you to experience them in every which way you prefer in every moment of your life.

This misunderstanding is mainly due to the powers of religious righteousness and authority which have been in control of humanity on earth for a very, very long time. These powers are the powers of the collective darkness of ego consciousness. They entertain the idea that you yourself are not in control of your destiny, your future, or of your own life. Instead you are led to believe that you are living in the hands of some kind of outside power that is meting out its reward or punishment on every occasion when you need to make a choice. It's no wonder that you are indeed afraid of changes.

This leaves you unable to choose change, unable to choose new directions for yourself, because you are so afraid of the consequences in an unknown future. But you see, at every crisis that you are given, that you have given yourself, you have in truth come to a cross-roads where you can turn your life around. You can do this whether you acknowledge that it is you who has instigated the crisis, or whether you feel that it is somebody else's choices which have forced you into a personal turmoil.

Turn your own conditioning around, because it is that very

conditioning from the past which has brought you into the here and now, and, if you do not change it, you will go on and create the same conditioning into the future too.

You will even get to suffer more in the future, if you have suffered in the past and are unwilling to try a new approach which can turn your experiences around from negative action to positive re-action. In the crisis, in the middle of the here and now, you are in the position of being able to create a new future for yourself. All you need to do is to throw away the past patterns, the conditioning which is based on your previous experiences and which has placed you in this behaviour pattern.

In that very moment, in the crisis, you may turn inwards. Stop looking at yourself with eyes toward the mirror that only reflects your appearance and your achievements, and instead go within. Turn away from the distracting chatterbox of your thoughts, into the silence, into the darkness of the unrecognised, into the unknown part of yourself, and start to get to know the inner self which is satisfied just by being.

Then you may start to discover the peace and harmony that is within your seventh heaven, within the dimension where all is one, and where 'one self' is everything. And so that is your divine gift to yourself, to be able to rediscover this part of yourself while you are still physically alive; instead of going through the transition of death and thereby needing to come back to earth in order to complete a final lifetime with this experience.

Many angelic souls have come to earth with the intention of doing this just once; just stepping down there once to see for themselves what it is like, getting into the density of physical matter, into the material world, and starting to feel the experience of earth's gravity, the pulling weight of heavy matter of which the physical earth consists. But in doing this they have got stuck in the process.

They have found that their 'wings' have become burdened with the thought of sin, of guilt, the loss of understanding of their ability to be their own creator. And instead, they have given in to the authority in power on earth, to the forces of ego which controls for its own benefit; the benefits of greed, power, money, possessions, all resulting in people being enslaved to a master.

Now I really want to remind you of the precious gift which is yours and which is within your own life, your own hands, and your own heart. This is your own power. Because you see, many, many have discovered, when they came over to this other side and finally 'found' themselves and their true nature of being, that their physical life which they had just discarded was indeed what they really wanted, but had not known how to appreciate.

What deserves appreciation is life's wonderful possibility to create yourself anew, to change, to transform, to be able to enjoy the earthly pleasures with the knowledge of the heart, and with the security of love in the heart.

It is not the nature of the heart to see everything in duality, in black and white, or to judge itself, to seek precedence or make itself subservient to another. It is the nature of pure hearts to be innocent; to be as children who are playing on the playground, eagerly experiencing, understanding and learning from every challenge they meet and go through.

The children from the heavens assimilate into their whole being every new skill they learn or step they take going forward; as well as picking themselves up when they fall in the process of teaching themselves how to walk independently. Every new sound, every new dance, every new person they get to know is met with excitement. And this is how you could live on earth, and how you are hopefully going to be manifesting in a new era called 'The Golden Age'. This has been promised when love consciousness, or Christ Consciousness, returns to earth. And this is going to happen in the next millennium.

You are at the threshold, and as you are the people who are going to transcend and to transform, to become the change on earth, you have a great deal of responsibility on your shoulders. But you will also find that you still have your angel wings. They will grow in the shape of your psychic powers, and these will start to serve you as soon as you start to get a new and divine opinion of yourself and the meaning of your life.

Because being given the breath of life is not meant to be a punishment. You are truly being given a great honour that is yours to discover from within. And when you start to put this sort of value on your life, you will also start to put the same value on the life of every one else. In consequence, you will find it impossible to take life, to kill or to go to war, because the respect for life will come from within, from your own understanding; and from that place you will awaken and ride into the sunrise, commencing a millennium of peace on earth.

In the meantime, there will be a need for some peace makers to come your way, to show you this new path of all-encompassing love, and through it the necessary understanding between peoples and nations of a new world order based on love, and not on greed for money and control. Because there will still be a tough fight between collective ego consciousness and soul consciousness, between the lower and higher consciousness, and this is what the biblical predictions of a war of evil versus good are all about.

The old ways of limited thinking will come to an end at the turn of this new millennium. Instead, there will be a new beginning for life, one that offers a combined spiritual and divine scientific understanding of the self and the universe. You see, all of the principles of The Divine, The One Infinite Creator, are built on mathematics, on sacred geometry and universal law.

Do not think, however, that there have to be many lives lost, or that it need come to dramatic changes like some continents becoming submerged and others rising. You are all responsible for the way this develops. By opening up to your heart consciousness, by simply turning within and meeting yourself from love and not from the point of fear and judgement, the change can be accomplished. And this is my gift to you, to come back and remind you of the path to truth, and I know and fully appreciate that my work can be continued as I speak.

It is very much a matter of the heart for me, that you should understand the importance of this message that I am bringing forth now. And I will use my own life as a perfect example for you; as I was meant to be an example for you, I still am.

You see, in my life as Diana, Princess of Wales, I was not able to express my true self. I expressed the role of the Princess of Wales and therefore I got cheered as the Princess of Wales. All I did in public was to be the perfect actress in the role of the princess. And this is how I got my outward identity, how I got your adoration, how I got the attention of the world to start with.

But I was very, very unhappy with my self for not being able to be me and follow my heart, instead of the customs of the royal upper class. I was choking under the strain of my own feelings until I understood that I was in fact free to express my self if only I stopped fearing rejection. This, however, did not happen until I got out of the golden cage, presented with the key of marriage all expenses paid, that the royal family had given me.

However, then I was confronted by my own past choices every time I went outside my own door. The past attention was still keeping up with me, because I myself had chosen to become a public figure in the first place.

As you know, all the prestige, all the glamour and everything that came with the territory did not make me happy. On the contrary, you saw how I suffered, you saw it in my eyes, although most of the time I smiled. I smiled a lot and I behaved bravely as I did my best to act out the character of the lonely princess in which I had cast myself. Wedding the Prince was my own greatest wish come true, my dream from when I was a teenage girl. So how can I complain? I only got what I wanted; only I did not know what that implied, what was in store for me.

I only started to find some meaning in my life when I stopped identifying with Her Royal Highness, and instead got in contact with the inner royalty of the child Diana: the inner child who lived all by itself inside of me, who was yearning for love, unconditional love for Diana, and not just because of my royal acting.

So I started bringing that inner part out. I brought out the natural capacity you all have, the capacity for empathy, for compassion, when I began my charity work for others, caring for the less fortunate in society. And I found that in this way I could also start to care for the poor 'weak', hurting part of myself, my own vulnerability. Seemingly, the part opposed to the 'strength', the self-control that is so much cherished in your society.

This is how all of you could get in contact with the lost part of yourselves. The part that is the divine child expressing its love, a virtue which got suppressed when you started finding your specific role models in life, and learning your lines while you went through 'acting' school.

You put on the masks in order to satisfy your surroundings, to get the applause; and the applause became the measurement of your own perceived success. It started at school when you worked for good grades, it continued as you competed for the best-paid jobs and climbed the social ladder to success.

All of you who are on this road, scaling this ladder of social acceptance at the expense of your self, know that it doesn't bring happiness; it only brings more loneliness as you distance yourself further and further from that inner loving part of yourself. And that is the inner expression of sensitivity and vulnerability, of innocence and pure joy.

Innocence is the true nature of who you are. When you are innocent, you have not started to judge yourself for good or bad behaviour, a judgement which brings forth guilt. And the guilt complex, the guilt that is following you throughout your lives, is your worst enemy because this guilt is formed from the perception of all the 'shoulds' and 'if onlys'. These concepts are influencing you, so that you will never be satisfied with what you have, if you are always focusing on what you are lacking.

Instead, start to be grateful for all that you have now in your life. Not necessarily for what you have achieved, but for those special moments, those glimpses of being in harmony with your self that you have had throughout the day; when you didn't have to act as someone else, when you didn't have to climb the ladder and be paid for your work.

The moment to treasure is when you can just be, and be true to yourself just by being who you are without judgement; that's the moment to expand, so that you can start to live in the mode of inner trust and safety and harmony and peace within your self.

Look within, listen within and the answers will come. Not as a 'should have', 'could have', or 'ifs' or 'buts'. No, just sit within your breathing, sit within your self in the moment of stillness, in a moment of meditation. For it is only by going within that you can find the light that is keeping you alive, the light that is bringing you love and gratification; not by doing, but by being.

That love and that light and the reality of that being are available to you at any moment of your life – if you choose to listen within.

This is your own choice. You need to take into your heart the understanding that you do have a choice. And the only choice you need to be concerned about is whether you want to be in harmony with your self, or whether you want to be in the confusion which is caused by fear; and so need to work through all the different manifestations which this fear is presenting to you.

The only choice you need to consider carefully is the choice between reacting from love or reacting from fear to every event which happens in your life. For when you choose from love, you choose from your true nature, from your heart; when you choose from fear, you choose from the authorities outside of yourself who have fed you with low self-esteem and a general mistrust in your own abilities for mastery. So go see for yourself, and the truth shall set you free.

 Chapter 8

I would like to speak to you about the subject of rejected love. You all know of this, it is part of your experience. It is part of the human experience of love. And most of you never seem to forget those who rejected your love which you offered. However, you tend to forget about those whom you rejected for the same purpose.

You tend to choose love that is unavailable because to you this seems to have the greatest market value. Besides, isn't it only natural that somebody does not love you, since you think you don't deserve love? Because if you don't love yourself, you cannot expect that the person of your dreams will love you, until you yourself admit to the very qualities that you seek in another.

This is part of the scheme which you discover within yourself. What you find attractive is what you are denied. What you want, you cannot have. It is like this already with children. Just look what happens when they are denied their wishes. They scream "I want, I want!" And you continue to grow by this model, this model of being attracted to the forbidden, to the unavailable. No mystery though, since this is the drive that at all times ensures your further.

The thought that 'the grass is always greener on the other side of the fence, or in some other field,' is also part of your over-all understanding. It is part of your universal search for the ulti-mate; in order to make you move on, instead of your evolution standing still.

You can never be satisfied with what you have for very long, because you need to get on with your search, and you need to get hold of something that is hanging high, nearly out of reach, in order to feel that you have succeeded.

This whole rejection paradigm is due to the fact that you con-nect love with fear; a constant fear of losing the love you have found, once you have found it. And the fear of love prevails in most of you. Of course it is understandable. This is part of your agenda and you tend to constantly experience rejection from those you love the most.

If in childhood you have not already felt rejection from your parents, you can be pretty sure it will show up as you grow into puberty. You fall in love and discover that your love is not returned, and so you get your first heartache, and then perhaps the second and then the third, and thus it continues.

It also has to do with the interaction between your soul and your ego, the 'I want' consciousness which does not necessarily agree with what your soul is seeking out for your learning experience.

Many of you, or I should really say 'us', do not really recover from these early disappointments. You keep on repeating the patterns of disappointment because the energy charge which comes from what you fear the most is exactly what is going to be returned to you as your very own experience. Remember what I have said, that thoughts and energies sent out in the past are what will be manifesting as your future.

In your relationships, you repeat your previous disappointment because you fear being rejected again, and thus you expect further disappointments. You repeat the negative pattern until you change your thoughts, your expectations about love – and the relationship to yourself.

Begin to trust that your 'luck' will change, that you can now start to receive love, and then your further experiences will lead you towards fulfilment of your wishes. I know this myself from the latter part of my life as Diana. If this is your agenda, it takes courage, it takes patience, and it means a lot of work with yourself, but it is surely worth it in the end.

The happiness I finally experienced with Dodi makes up for many of the unhappy years, because you see, it is not quantity of time that matters, it is quality that counts when you look back. Time is only a measurement of linear experience.

This pattern of rejection is of course also due to previous life experience, because you tend to meet again those with whom you have unfinished business. Those that you have rejected in a previous lifetime seek you out in this lifetime and make sure that this debt is repaid to you, so the both of you can feel the other side of the coin. Thereby the energy between you is balanced out. Your karmic situation has been resolved.

Now, understand that this is really what makes relationships so difficult, because the love you are seeking from each other is not unconditional. It is in fact conditioned by, let's say, what you can get in return for the love that you give. You may be evaluating each other in such a way that you both may be meeting with a business proposition, instead of giving a gift from your hearts.

This usage of 'love' leads you into pain and sorrows, into divorces and new relationships all the time, because you think that changing partners will help, instead of realising that the problem is not with the partner, the problem is within yourself. Instead of realising this, you will be looking around, perhaps looking back at your past, and thinking that something is wrong with you because you do not see the workings of your patterns, that you are caught in a destructive behaviour pattern.

This pattern may perhaps not be understood until a much later stage in your life. As you grow from experience, you gain wisdom, you seek out the answers to your questions. And this is part of the agenda which you all are seeking, a search for a deeper meaning because you understand that the love you know now is not the answer to your dreams, the answer to your endless prayers.

All of you are longing to be loved without conditions, without having to pay or get paid for the exchange of this so-called feeling, this precious state of being.

What you are all longing for is the totality of love that comes from a loving parent who loves you for who you are, just by being their precious beloved child.

The Creation Mother/Father God loves you this way, but the only person that can give you this love is yourself to yourself, and within yourself you can find this love fulfilled, as you develop your relationship with God within.

All the time you evolve, you are stretching yourself towards a greater love, and with this love comes the gift of seeing the true quality of love, not as merchandise or something you trade in order to gain something, or to add value to yourself. But you start to see love as a flowing energy that you tap into and which has a source that is never going to empty, because love is indeed an energy that is recycling and can fill you up over and over again.

This is indeed the meaning of the search for The Holy Grail. You are seeking a way back to the youthful source of love, the source of The Creator. Sadly, many of you do not understand The Creator. Or let's say, the picture you have of The Creator is such that you do not see and understand yourself as The Creator. I would like to give you an example of how you might view yourself as God the Creator as well as the creation.

You, your evolution, is all happening within a circle placed within a sphere. You yourself are becoming the circle, as you are both the beginning and the end, going around in a circle in order to get back to yourself.

At the beginning of linear time, in a big bang occurrence, the Star Creator decided to become the creation in order to experience itself. Commencing out of an implosion of the Great Central Sun in antimatter which left a black hole in space, he/she exploded into matter through many, many light fragments of the One. The One became you, and then you, the light of your soul, started out on a long, long journey.

This journey took you far away from your heavenly birthplace as you moved into a cycle in circular motion, going further and further down along the line away from the source of your creation. And as you went on, you put on more and more density, the light weakened, you forgot about your divine heritage, you forgot who and what you were. You did this in order to experience separation from the source. On the way you fragmented further into many more pieces of yourself, which went on as independent parts of the 'One of the One' you all once were.

Finally, at some time or another, after arduous trials, you will 'find your self' totally confused at the exact opposite point of the circle, in total darkness. Then all of a sudden, at the darkest moment of your life, you finally look inwards and in a divine revelation you get a glimpse of the opposite side. The bright light from your source will hit you, and from then on it will start giving you enlightenment in order to show you the path back to the source of oneness. Joyfully you can now start to travel away from the darkest point of your life's circle and go towards the light on the opposing side.

You can observe this concept in the ancient esoteric symbol of Yin and Yang. One half of the circular sphere is light and the other half is darkness. You always travel back from darkness into the light again. But then, understand that there will always be a point of darkness within the light, a black hole, to remind you of the opposite side of the creation, the duality. And there will always be a point of light in all the darkness in order to direct you back to the source of light.

Never forget the wholeness, the understanding that The Creator, as you, are both the darkness and the light combined. Because you know, as happens with anything that gets lighted up only on one side, there is another side as well, and even if the light is not there to show it to you at this time, it is still part of the same creation.

So your journey is one where you move away from the Source just to discover that you have gone as far as you could, and then you start on your way back home again. And this is what your evolution is all about. And for every time that you do the circle, and for every time that you meet up with the fragments that were lost on the way, you become more whole.

As you go in a spiralling movement throughout the circle, you gain more and more knowledge, more and more wisdom, and the wisdom you have gained on your trip away from the source, you use as you go back. You use it to teach the others that you meet on your way, those who are coming down the opposite route, in the circle's other direction, moving away from their light. At this part of the path you become the master, teaching those who are in search of themselves. Most human beings still do not know that they will finally bite their own tail.

This analogy of the snake is an ancient holy symbol of the God essence: the snake biting itself in its tail in order to achieve completeness. And the force that is leading you onwards on this journey is truly the force of the internal snake, the kundalini energy, the energy that runs through your spine and keeps the different energy centres, the chakras, working and in place within your energy system.

There are seven chakras, and these are the centre-points of the energy flow. They run throughout the fields of the different energy bodies, measuring and maintaining your physical, emotional, mental and spiritual balance at all times. And the balance you seek is found in the balance of the rainbow-coloured spectrum of light, and the balance of the scale of musical notes. These are also represented by the chakras and respond synchronously through the spine.

There is much healing that can and will be done in the future through knowledge of the spectrum of sound and the spectrum of colour. Because colour and sound penetrate directly through to the core of your being, the spine, where the root of physical, emotional and mental problems arise. There will be much more forthcoming in order to teach you; however, there are already other sources that provide information on this matter. I only wanted to give you some background for further study.

Indeed I do study a lot; I am now getting enrolled in a 'celestial university class' where I get a lot of information, and some of this information I am trying to relate back to you. But you see, when we are at this stage of evolution, we are not necessarily communicating by words, but by knowledge applied through an experience of energy. Therefore I need to use my expertise (!) with earthly words as I try to transmit in physical terms the understanding of what I am learning and the knowledge of what I am experiencing.

This is not always easy, but in this way you at least get an idea, so that you will not be unprepared for further evolution in the understanding of physical bodies, along with the energy bodies that complete your being. With my learning I also get treatment, and I get to work with energy.

I am told that I will also at some point be able to transmit healing energy through to you as well. As you read my words you will be able to feel my vibrations, and as you listen to my spiritual voice, carrying my energy imprint, you will be able to open up to an energy frequency that will be responding from within yourselves. And this is a gift that Sananda, Jesus the Christ, is relaying through my channel and me.

This however is only in the commencing stage, and both I and my channel will need to develop this ability further, and go into a training program so that this can be done within the boundaries of physical manifestation, when time and space allows it to occur.

I thank you for the patience you are showing by reading this book, although you may wonder about its content, its thoughts, and about me and the channel that is bringing it forth. Do not hesitate to ask within yourself, to ask your heart, and your heart will tell you what to believe. Through its discrimination, the sense of well being, peace and harmony, the heart always tells you the truth.

# Part 2

## *Higher Education*

# Chapter 9

I have just come back from class, mind you. I have finally started the higher intellectual education that I felt I lacked while I lived on earth as Diana. However this kind of intellectual universal understanding requires an emotional intelligence as well, and it is different because it covers the wholeness of things, of being, a universal understanding that you don't get in your earthly classrooms.

Up until now you have decided to focus mainly on the third dimensional existence, so that you may live in the self-made reality that you have constructed in order to learn from each other through the aspect of time.

But in order to learn about yourselves from yourselves, you need to go to a different level of perception, and of learning and teaching. And this is what the present stage of evolution is going to ensure. The people on earth are going to get the opportunity to grow and learn 'en masse'.

All of you are participants in the 'New Age' movement through time and space, whether you want it, and whether you realise it or not.

I started to learn a few things myself while I was living amongst you; however, I was too busy coping with my daily problems to ever think along the lines of universal problem solving. However, as I am now able to have some overview and some perspective, I am coming into a position to be able to give you further advice along the way. This includes a certain perception of what is going on in-between worlds, in addition to the physical school of reality where you have enrolled yourselves.

For instance, one thing that I want to mention is that the leadership which is finally going to evolve on earth is the kind that will produce leaders who are going to lead others to master themselves. The pupils will then learn to master their own future, master their reality, and then become leaders in their own right.

The leadership that is going to lead you into the future is the leadership of heart, where the understanding is that of mastery through the power of love. The power of love is not filled with fear of losing, filled with competition. The power of love only wishes to share and give, and thereby renew itself all the time. For the source of love is that of continuing cycles, and in the process of giving yourself to love, you will discover that fear is indeed a self-constructed illusion.

You are what you are thinking. Whatever is your perception of yourself and your life, you are becoming that at all times. And when you start to desire change, and need change, and think of change and further development, you begin evolving to another level of perception where you decide to reclaim your power, and keep it for yourself instead of giving it away.

You have become experts in giving your personal power away to all kinds of outer distractions. You give it to all the games that you play, to the sports that illustrate your eagerness to compete, to entertainment and alcohol and drugs, media or computer obsession, you name them, all the kinds of disturbances that keep you away from thinking, and learning from within yourself.

Instead of keeping yourself from awareness that earth is just a little part of something much grander, learn about the path of the soul and the ways of the universe: vast in truth, since the multitude of other civilisations is far-reaching throughout the universe.

However, up until now you have decided to stay ignorant. This is your common decision, whereby you have given your personal power away to a leadership outside of yourself: the leadership of money, the power of wealth, and the power of outer riches, instead of the richness of inner wisdom and peace.

The peace that you seek, the end of war between the nations and peoples of earth, you will not be able to accomplish until you achieve peace with yourselves. And this is where all of you can contribute because, when you make peace within yourself, you have an immense power. You are not powerless people. All of you individuals have the possibility to aspire to greatness beyond all expectations.

You have all possibilities within you, and it is only the range of your thinking that puts limits to your realising this. Look at the countless examples where just one person has helped to change the way the world perceives things. And I want to show you that this can also be the case for yourself.

When you decide to get together in order to stand together, to stand up for your own thoughts, feelings and opinions, then you are going to become the new authority in the world. And this authority of yours will not tolerate injustice, will not tolerate dishonesty or corruption, because you know that you have to pay back for everything that you inflict on others. So you will start to choose to inflict only love, and then you will become the love and peace you are seeking for yourselves.

Wars amongst nations show you the war of your own inner workings, of your own disharmony between mind and heart, between love and fear. And when you work on your inner progress, as I suggest you commit yourself to do, then your spirit will enter and provide all the help you can need.

But understand, it may not perhaps be always in the way you want, or think that you want, because the spirit will always give you the help that you truly need there and then. And that help is not based on the fear of lack, coming from the ego, but comes in the form of the courage of your soul. So whatever situation you find yourself in, know that you have something to learn.

Know that you have decided, in agreement with your soul, to put yourself into this situation, so stop blaming anyone or anything outside of yourself. Because blaming others is how you have given up your power, by thinking that somebody else is in charge of your future, your destiny, the events happening in your life; when in fact all the decisions inflicted on yourself have been made by your self, and you are living through them. This is the number one rule of self-development, to admit to your own responsibility in all the workings of your life.

You learn to observe your thoughts and not become a victim of your mind. In directing your thought, you start to realise the very process of creating.

Remember what it says in the Bible that you know; 'In the beginning was the word and the word was with God... And the Light

shineth in darkness.' What this means is that before the beginning
of the universal existence, there was only stillness. Then there came
a ripple in the stillness that made vibrations. And the vibrations
turned into frequencies that started to swirl around in a circle, spiralling in increasing speed and making high pitched frequencies of
sound. Which then, because of the incredible speed, made light;
and the light created by the sound started to create matter, becoming a sun, 'the Great Central Sun', the main source of energy that is
bringing The Light outwards.

This was the beginning of the creation of the sparks of light
that became you. And remember that the sound became words,
and that the words became thoughts, the original thoughts that
came from the movement of sound. That sound is thought, and
thought makes sound, ripples of energy being sent out into the
ether. And therefore you create by sound, which makes up words
from thought.

The light, which is the speed of sound/thought, contains the
spectrum of the colours. These colours are the different frequencies of speeding light. The light is moving through space in countless different colour frequencies, but the light and the colour are
one and the same, divided into a spectrum of different frequencies,
or speeds of light.

The colours then become your emotions because light moves
through different octaves of sound as it interacts with your
thoughts, and from the spectrum of thought and spectrum of
coloured light came the energy charge which you call emotions.
And in fact, you may experience emotions as different colours within your body.

The energy behind the intensity of your feelings is the different speeding colours within your physical universe, and within the
physical spectrum of your body.

If, for instance, you would take a look at your body through a
microscope, you would find the most wonderful patterns of colours
building up the substance of your biological body. The molecules,
the different building blocks of your physical minerals, make a
beautiful work of art because everything is regulated within your
body, everything is built up in perfect mathematical order; although
your inherited fear of fear is disrupting the original order and

turning the body into disorder, into disease.

The irony is that what you fear most of all – the fear of chaos in a world of order – is precisely what causes chaos. But you have deluded yourself. Chaos is an illusion, because, when you trace all the chaos back into its component particles, you find that they consist of tiny simple parts of a particular order called fractals.

The exact order in the build-up of fractals demonstrates that the continual duplication of fractals of order produces chaos by its very magnitude, so that it looks complicated and chaotic. It is just being generated into plural chaos so that the chaos can be redirected to find its way back into singular order again. (Oops, is this making you feel dizzy?)

Chaos is caused when order multiplies itself. It may look like a disaster, but the disorder of chaos hides the realisation of perfect order, and this will manifest itself once again. Such is your life in the third dimension. You have created chaos in order to return to simplicity, and in order to realise the source behind the apparent turmoil. Because that source is a source of creativity – your own thoughts – and you yourself have created the chaos in order to show yourself different possibilities. And with different possibilities, you needed to create the illusion of time.

Because time is something that binds the events together. While you move through time, you become time yourself, through the events that happen to you and through you: so really, you are what is measured by time and not time itself. You are continuously growing and evolving through the events which are happening in your evolving life.

However, you still tend to think that birth is the beginning of your life. After you are born, you start to grow up, and then in the middle years you start to decay until it is over, as you know it, when you physically die. This is the physical life process you are measuring by a lifetime, or a life span. But understand that you yourselves are the ones who have differentiated the events to be measured into years, and the years into months and the months into days and the days into hours, and so on.

You have together decided the amount of seconds, minutes, hours, days, months and years, as the measurement used in your society. While in other societies, or previous societies like the old culture of the Maya Indians, there were different ways of counting time. And the Chinese people have a different way of counting the years of time even now.

So you can see that time is a question of perception. It is a way to measure events so that they can occur in due order, to separate events so that they do not become chaotic. And thus you may learn from action and reaction.

When you understand that you yourself are fabricating the time that makes everything happen in your life – at your own pace, in your own time and your own space – you also start to become aware of the possibility of stopping time. Or of making time go slower and making time go faster, by speeding up or slowing down the development of your life through your decisions.

You probably all have known how this feels; when, for instance, you are in a trance-like state of being, such as when you are doing art work like painting or another activity that is really engulfing you. Then you may feel that time is standing still, and it is indeed, because you become totally focused in the moment and thereby stretch the perception of the experience.

The expansion or contraction of time is an experience that you will feel more and more often in the future. It is getting closer and closer to your consciousness because this is what the earthly evolution is all about. You are to surpass time and go through to the inner space of your universe and tap into your own inner understanding.

This also leads us to the event which at this point is destined to commence around year 2012. Since time is not made of matter, but occurs through the influence of the decisions of thought-energy flowing between all of you, including the consciousness of mother earth itself, it is impossible to give an exact point of time for events to come. And indeed this goes for all kinds of predictions.

However, I have now been given permission to speak to you about this upcoming event. And this is what all these reflections have been leading up to. Because it is indeed the end of time as you know it. It is not only the end of previous behaviour, but also the beginning of the new understanding at a heightened level of perception and of experience.

You will, for instance, get to experience more and more in the upcoming years a feeling of déjà-vu, of precognition, of being in a situation which you feel you have lived in before. Because you can start going back and forth in time to the degree that you choose to open up to the inner perception of 'no time'. And then you can also become an observer of time, rather than a participant.

This means that you can relive a particular situation and experience it once more. But, if you have changed in the meantime, you can also get a different outcome from this same situation. Then you become a creator in a so-called 'lucid' time frame. If this sounds confusing, you just may want to wait and see what comes as you go on. But you cannot steer away from this expansion of your perceptions. It is truly part of the common evolution, and indeed it will become the revolution of the times.

Another thing to consider is the major 'flap' regarding the year 2000 in the field of computer technology. You should know that despite constant flexibility and the evolution of technology in the computer world at large, you have only lately 'remembered' that your computer programs were not pre-programmed to register beyond year 2,000. But this is not merely accidental; it is a result of the common semiconscious knowledge which you all have programmed into your DNA, the knowledge that the time frame will indeed change and thus mark an end and a new beginning around the year 2000.

Because this is the year when this change is set to be, let's say, common knowledge to all. And this is also part of my work at this time, to be able to continue to work from behind the scenes and give you some perspective, and hopefully also give you directions to lead you into freedom. Freedom from the time/space continuum on the physical earth so that you can leave the incarnation cycles in the third dimension, so you become masters yourselves. You are to be the masters of your own destiny instead of being victims of the delusions of the duality, which is the structure of the third dimension.

If we continue onwards for another 12 years, we approach the event happening as micro technology comes to a point of development where it meets the border of passing through the speed of light. And your technological development will keep on speeding towards this major event. However, according to your scientific computer experts you will then run up against a brick wall, making any further evolution impossible.

Understand that this is indeed the very wall that is separating the two dimensions. But this is by no means the finite end to speed itself. As you proceed through the light, you are truly becoming part of the light yourself, and have to, let's say, go with the flow – go where the light takes you. And the light will speed you into a spiralling vortex of timelessness, and then this vortex will speed you out into space, and cause you to disappear from physical perception as you see it now.

This is also what Einstein, your mathematics genius, tried to experiment with: to make objects invisible by speeding them into another time frame, or other dimension. However he did not have all the information available to him to accomplish this experiment successfully.

For a start, you should know that you cannot pass through time without being confronted by your spiritual nature. As you are confronted by 'the Light' you will indeed be requested to say yes or no, to deny or accept it. But I want to give you the perspective on your upcoming choice and its consequences. Because this is a choice that you will all need to make within yourselves and within the community as whole. You may, by the way, term this as Judgement Day for humanity.

And you do have the examples to choose from. You have them closer than you think. Because the examples are the visitors from outer space who are already within your reality, but most of you are ignorant, or choose to be ignorant, of this fact. And the choice they are showing you is to develop either through technological mind power or through love power. Through the power of high tech instrumental technology at the expense of love or through the power of universal light technology based on the knowledge of love.

The agenda is as follows: either you become technical super humans and thereby can make high-tech mind technology based on artificial intelligence, and go on expeditions to other worlds with technology corresponding to your own – and this means Star Wars in its full scope. Because, like yourselves, these other communities are only going to be looking out for their own interests, and so you will again be meeting yourselves with the same weapons. And this is the weapon of fear.

This scenario is that of many science fiction movies and novels, and these worlds that meet you with fear are those of the various monsters – the ones resembling the different cartoon characters. They are real for a fact – if you choose that delusion as reality.

The other option you are given is the opposite one, to choose to admit to your divine nature and to the divine oneness of all. And this is the true reality, because darkness is the illusion belonging to the thoughts of the ego mind. This other choice is to acknowledge your divine heritage and go with the flow of the universal will, which will lead you back to its own womb, back to its light, back to its divine love.

All humanity knows this truth within their hearts, and that is why I am asking you to listen to your inner truth; to listen to what your intuition says, and not what the outer society will say about what I have come to tell you. You see, you are all part of my consciousness, and I am also part of yours. So you need to listen within, whether what I have to tell is the truth for you, or whether it isn't.

I have come back to show you the path to your own inner truth, and not to tell you to follow my truth. We are all responsible for our individual truth because that is our purpose for living, for existing, to come back to the source with our information, our own true stories, and thus merge our light bodies with the source of all light, all information, all sound, all colours. And thereby we enrich the universe and make it an even more beautiful creation, and so it expands and expands and expands, and it is never ending, its possibilities are endless.

The last time you had this choice was many, many thousands of years ago, in the time that contained the experience of Atlantis, or Atlan-ta as it was also called. Your souls know of this continent, although it was lost from history because this happened before your written stories, as you know them.

However, you were participants then, and in the evolution of

your society at that time you made the decision to go with the technology instead of a creation made from love, the love consciousness which you had as heritage from an even earlier continent
called Lemuria. And this time around, you are confronted with your
decisions from back then.

You had the technology, the same as you will have this time,
although with some differences. You had the technology to alter
genes and DNA. You were splitting DNA and splicing genes and creating your own creatures, for instance those which were half human
and half animal. You were creating by cloning and you were creating by sound, and you were using colours as a mode of healing, for
instance by laser light. And these possibilities are also going to be
presented to you now. It is already starting to happen, as the inven-
tions will reappear from within your own minds. (Perhaps now you
can understand the massive protests throughout the world against
cloning and gene modification)

Because you see, you are to relive Atlantis. As it was foretold in
the prophecies, Atlantis will rise again; however not from the bottom of the sea, not from the floor of the oceans, but from the
expansion of your mind. As it was overthrown at one time by your
suppressed emotions, it is going to arise again from your emotions.
(A huge wall of water, caused by a giant 'technological' explosion,
drowned the ancient continent and thereby destroyed the prosper-
ous Atlantean evolution).

If you choose to go in the same direction as before, you will
experience a destruction once again; but this time it would be a
total destruction because now the Atlanteans have come to inherit
the whole world, and so the destruction – if you choose to go the
Atlantean way – would be total.

If, on the other hand, you choose to go further back in your
heritage and regain the knowledge of Lemuria, you will enter the
prophesied 1000 years of evolution in harmony and love, and make
earth a heavenly place for future generations to inherit. (The continent of Lemuria was built on 5th dimensional love, empowered and
realised by living in harmony and understanding with all the elements and all creation on earth).

If you choose this, you will start to interact with the other
beings of the universe that have evolved through the evolution of

love. By choosing love, you will start to interact with the extraterrestrial brothers and sisters who are coming to you with the offer of love and peace, and you get to enjoy their light technology which they will willingly share with their younger earth siblings.

But as long as you have an international governmental 'treaty', signed in London back in 1947, you cannot expect them to freely come and show themselves, as a general rule just to die a martyr's death,. This document instructs all governments and top military units around the world to destroy and keep secret whoever or whatever they might capture which is of an extraterrestrial nature.

Nonetheless, living extraterrestrials have been captured. And it has happened in order to try to demonstrate the peace and benevolence of these friends, but you still respond to them with hostility. You answer with fear. And the way you answer their appearance in earth's atmosphere is simply to shoot them down with laser rocket missiles, officially meant for satellites.

This is the usual way you communicate and settle differences between yourselves; you go to war and kill off what you feel is a threat coming from the outside. This is indeed but an outer image of your own fear of communicating with the unknown parts of your inner selves; be those your feelings of love, tenderness, jealousy, bitterness, hatred, sorrow, pain or frustration.

But the real potential is that of love consciousness, instead of mind without heart. And that is what is going to become your new and true reality, because it is seen as your highest potential, and indeed the potential that is the overwhelmingly probable outcome.

It always has been, because although the power of darkness has the possibility of ruling, it will never have the possibility of over-ruling the light when light is chosen. And this is the nature of the current experience of earth, that you go through darkness in order to choose light and love. And because it is the overall experience, it is the experience of each and every one of you.

You are all bonded together. You are in fact being presented with the same set of lessons throughout your lives, but at different time intervals. And therefore you do not always see the similarity, because the circumstances you are placed in differ in order that you may evolve as fragments of the whole.

If you only experienced your similarities, you would not have the friction caused by your differences which you need to grow. For instance, you may therefore find yourselves in families that seem alien; you feel like a stranger who, in your opinion, might as well have been adopted into the family.

You may feel the disharmony in your life as a punishment, instead of understanding that it is a way of evolving through differences and difficulties in order to find your own inner strength; to get courage and thereby be able to see the light within yourselves – and choose the path of light for your future.

I have finally been able to 'pick up' those New Age books that I left behind. Books containing the esoteric knowledge that I was seeking on earth, but was too busy to be able to look into, because I could not think at the same time that I was being overwhelmed with pre-programmed emotions. For you see, this is why you have to balance yourselves. You need to balance emotions with intellect, because the light of colours and the music of sound is going to free you, through the ability to communicate your feelings to yourself and then to others. To be able to express your self without the fear of rejection is finally going to set love free.

Honest communication and acceptance of self is going to heal you. The possibilities inherent within this evolution will set you free and become the cure for many of your physical diseases, as well as mental and emotional disease.

All this is going to give you a picture of wholeness and you will feel that it is magic, not understanding that it is the mathematics of the order which is consistent throughout the universe, the order of logic through emotion and emotion through logic.

In order to find what the mathematicians are searching for, which is 'the super formula', you have to look within and find within yourselves the order of consciousness through balance and harmony. This is the formula that will divulge the construction of the universal intelligence, the formula that will give you final proof of order in the universe.

This is because your universe within is a microscopic copy of the universe at large. And thus, by finding the solution to your own, let's say, peace with yourself, you will be able to connect with the harmony of the spheres.

The harmony of the spheres is the harmony which is being emitted from yourselves when you have realised yourselves and connected within yourself, and thereby become one with the outer and the inner self. And thereby become the light and the music, and once again travel on waves of love back into your creator.

 Chapter 10

After the intellectual and scientific nature of the last exercise, I think we all of us need a break. So let us go back to the issues of emotions and my present condition. And the way I see my life from this perspective.

Regarding my personal life however, I am not going to go into the depths, not in this book anyway. But you understand, I still want to express some of the emotions that I have gone through during this present period of realisation.

As I look back at my life at this point, I am indeed happy to be where I am now. However, it is still with a pang of grief, of sorrow and sadness within my heart, that I look down at my beloved sons, my earth family. And I have to say that a part of me still misses that part of my experience. To be able to cuddle and hug my little darlings, keep them close to me and feel the love of their hearts beating against mine. It was my mother love for them which they willingly returned, for I was indeed giving them all that I had to give in that department.

But after all, I must say that it has all worked out for the best, for the benefit of all. For my boys too, although this is difficult for you to see at this point, but the future will tell. Because they need this sad experience of loss in order to develop within their own path and gain the strength they need in order to make their decisions for the future.

Know that at this point of time I do not wish to comment much further on them, nor my relationship to them or to any of the men previously involved in my life. I have to consider their feelings, and the feelings of my late family and the royal family. This book is neither the time nor the place to reflect on personal family business.

What I am trying to do in this book, however, is to give you a perspective of myself as you, as a human being, versus what I am experiencing in the after life. And as the after life is a continuing experience of what was going on before in the previous life, I cannot say that I am totally freed from all sadness and emotional pain. However, I have learned to make use of the pain within the joy of my own development, through the experience of once again living through everything that was in store for me at that time.

When you get to look at your life in the the after life, which is like a mirror, you see all the points where you could have acted differently, or simply have behaved in another way in order not to inflict pain on others. For the pain that you inflict on others, you get to experience yourself as you review your life. Because this is the only way you learn 'post mortem'.

You see, you get to become the other person, get into the emotions of the receiver of your actions, so that you yourself can there and then feel their reactions to your actions. And thereby you are able to come to some conclusions and decisions on what your further learning experience will be in the time to come, in this dimension.

You should know that the dimensions are not really situated on top of each other like a ladder you climb step by step, or like several storied buildings of varying heights. No, the dimensions are all intertwining and they are sort of crossing and blending into each other, like spheres within spheres. And in such a way that everything actually exists in the same space but at different rates of speed. In this way we are hidden from each other, because our range of energies are not compatible; unless we step down our energies and you increase your energy level at the same time. That way we can meet in the middle.

This is actually how this connection, how this function of channelling, is working. To communicate in this way is a skill that my channel has acquired in her previous lifetimes, and I myself in my own past experience have been trained this way before.

Bear in mind that all that you have learned well in previous existences shows itself as talents in your present life; and these you can tap into and reuse if this is part of your life plan.

In my lifetime as Diana I was rather fascinated by fortune-tellers and the fact that it was possible to look into the future as well as into the past. And at this point I am able to understand something of the workings of these skills that psychics use to take a peek into upcoming events and the unknown. But the problem is that the outcome is always dependent on the ability of the medium, how they relate to the information in order to understand the symbols, and in turn translate the information to the person asking the questions.

This means that there is always a good risk that they misunderstand what is shown to them, whether they are cards or symbols, and thereby arrive at the wrong conclusions. And this is very dangerous indeed, because people tend to believe everything, every word that they hear, and then blindly follow the advice they are given.

The cards and predictions always have their basis in the situation here and now, and show the prognosis based on the assumption that in the future the people involved will keep on behaving in their regular, expected patterns. But people do change, and they do unexpected things all the time.

The path on which you are walking is in fact not a straightforward road, and time is not following a straight line. No, the 'time lane' is curving and bending in angles of every sort, and you certainly cannot always look around the next curve to see the next turn of events. Therefore, it is also impossible to estimate events exactly within a time frame. It bends to your choices and decisions all the time. And it is impossible to estimate the chances of any event, other than by prognosis of what is going to happen.

As you walk down the lane of time, you are setting your footprints every moment onto a path towards the future. Besides this, on the energy level you are all the time interacting with others who have an intention to cross your upcoming path. Together then, you are making future decisions that have to do with you and yourself, and you with them, and they with you.

But a decision taken in a moment can change things as you all move along; so what you get from the fortune-tellers is a picture of a possible future. And it may well be a future that never becomes reality, but disappears instead into a time loop because of all the conditions that have to be considered for it to be fulfilled.

It is very important that the psychics who advise people should tell them of upcoming events only as a future prognosis, based on all available information from the past; and that what they perceive may, and may not, become manifest in the future.

It is not very good for you to become dependent on fortune-tellers in order to make decisions and live your life. That way, you are no longer steering your life through free choice of your own will. You will instead be surrendering your own power, and be steered towards a given future which commenced in your subconscious feelings and thoughts, instead of relying on your conscious decisions at all times.

Your future can not be foretold to a 100 %, and there is always the question of interpretation and transcription. It was like this with me in my life, and it is so with the future of the world today.

Regarding the upcoming millennium shift, many people get caught up in the old scripts and prognoses from the past. Understand that instead of fearing destruction, you all have power to change your common future and make it a 'win, win' situation for all of you, and for the earth itself. The idea of destruction is what you read into the prophecies because you have not been able to understand what they really mean.

I have to give you some comments regarding my own previous experience with psychics and fortune-tellers because I was in fact foretold of a new beginning holding great love, great happiness and marriage and even a baby daughter to come in my near future. However, the 'readers' could not see the accident around the curve, because it was truly hidden in a time tunnel and was not about to reveal itself, although we did have some warnings of being accident-prone. But, you know, then I was not supposed to know and neither was anyone else.

In that sense, it is always The Creator or the higher guidance who puts together the schedule regarding our future, in accordance with a higher path and plan that serves not only yourself but is for the good of all.

In another way I have to say that the predictions were right, in the sense that I now am indeed experiencing being 'married' to heaven and earth. For at the same time that I am talking to you earthlings through a channel, an action which binds the dimensions together, I am residing here in the heavens or celestial dimensions. And here along with me is my soul twin as well as all the other soul mates, who altogether are becoming the new love of my life.

Indeed, you may say that the process of creating this book is the expected pregnancy; and that I am now delivering, in the spirit of the feminine soul, what is to become a new-born consciousness of the goddess on earth. And you will be the midwife of my 'child' as you receive my book of infinite love from the divine.

Now, the point that I wanted make clear is never to become too dependent on, let's say, clairvoyant readers. Because it is easy to give your power away to 'the cards' or to the astrological chart, instead of getting on with creating your life. You may use these things as directions, but you should know that you yourself are the player of the cards, the one who all the time deals the cards by giving them instructions through your sub-conscious, no matter who is physically putting them on the table. But please allow your conscious heart and higher mind to create from moment to moment.

The Tarot cards always show your emotions, picking up your thoughts which direct these emotions and vice versa. And by knowing this, you can steer away from unpleasant happenings as well as focus on a future that describes what you really want to happen. But know that the last word is going to be with The Creator within.

You should know also that each and every one of you has your own guardian angel or caretaker, and each of you also has an appointed guide, an advisor from the spirit world, who follows you from the day you incarnated on earth until you have arrived safely 'at home'. And these invisible helpers are doing everything in their power to steer you into the path of the heart. They help you in whatever circumstances you find yourself.

But you need to be willing to listen, and you need to trust your own intuition, because this is where you can feel the connection to these helping guardians and be able to listen to their advice by listening to your own feelings. Because, you see, you are not only experiencing your own feelings within your body, but you yourself are a whole energy system which is receiving inputs from others all the time, as well as sending out your energy as input to others.

You dispatch and receive energy in a constant flow through the chakras, your emotional centres, because the nature of your being is really a spiritual engine of energy. And the consciousness within your inner being is not confined only to your inner parts, it is indeed also spread throughout your personal auric field. This in turn is connected to the greater field that surrounds the planet earth, and this again is part of the sun system, the galaxies, and the universes in all the different dimensions.

Perhaps you perceive yourself as a human being who sometimes has spiritual adventures or experiences, while the truth is that you are indeed a spiritual being, a divine being of light that is having a physical experience on earth. And this distinction makes 'a world' of difference. Because you truly need to identify with the greater part of yourself, and not with your confinement within the physical body. Otherwise you will never be able to rise to your power and connect with that love which is your essence.

I would like to elaborate further regarding the issue of timing and predictions. Time is such an important matter, I feel. Because presently you are somewhat obsessed by time. You have so much to do all the time, and you try to fit it all into your daily lives by estimating the time for events and putting them into an agenda or schedule. And you probably even use a time manager in order to fit it all in.

But you see, if you could understand time, you would also be able to arrange your priorities differently; because you would understand that what you are doing is in fact trying to bypass time itself, by just 'passing time'. Instead of enjoying the time that you have at your disposal, during every day of your life on this planet.

This phenomenon is due to the times you live in. If you harbour the idea that your life is all over when it ends, it is understandable that you need to live everything at once and that you try to make the most out of those limited years of your life time. However, this results in your not being really present in any activity that you participate in. Try instead to start practising mindfulness in all activities. Stay with your experience and connect with it as you move through time.

Then instead, you can start to fully enjoy the time you have, enjoy the variety of all the different activities instead of just hurrying through the days. Your days need not be filled with stress and duties and work, always in fear of missing out on something. Know that everything has its own time. Perhaps you may choose some more free time for yourselves. I presume you have heard about 'having a good time'?

Bear in mind that experiencing and living is not achieved by getting everything done at once. Many of you connect happiness with duty. You feel that if you do your duty you will become happy. This is something that the old ways have instilled in you; all the feelings of responsibility, of duty - or of guilt if you are not spending all your time doing something useful. Instead you could be spending more and more time for your own pleasure, for your own inner self development, and thus find inner peace in no time. The time has come to lighten up and become joyful and happy by not taking yourselves and your lives so plain seriously all the time!

Another thing to watch is that it is so easy to get time-obsessed when it comes to predictions. Because if you get certain predictions and a time frame in which they seem likely to happen, you will most probably wait for this particular point in future-time instead of living in the here and now. Make the most out of every moment you have at your disposal, and little by little let the future become the now.

It is not very desirable to live in the future before that future becomes your living moment, because then you lose your ability to be satisfied with what you already have. Instead, you are looking over a fence towards a future that may seem greener from where you are, but you may not think so when you finally get there! 'New' problems may be arising then, obstacles that you do not perceive from your fence. Because you do have this terrific ability to keep on recreating the unsolved obstacles from the past and bringing them into the present - until you recognise your negative patterns and change them in the moment, here and now.

You see, it is so easy to place too many expectations on the future and thereby forget that you change on the way there, and that the future unfolds from what you are doing in the here and now. By counting your blessings, being happy and satisfied with what you now have in your life, accepting it and giving thanks for your situation as it appears in the present, you will ensure yourself happiness in the future also. If you manage to be grateful now, the future will take care of itself and give you more and more to enjoy.

You should know that what really matters is not what happens to you, but how you choose to react to what happens. That realisation may change your attitude towards life!

Now I wanted to emphasise the responsibility that any advisors, be they priests, psychologists, therapists, psychics or fortune-tellers, have towards the public, the people who are seeking answers from others. Because really, the only people that have the answers and can fully know what they want or need, are those persons themselves. Others can only act as advisers from their own point of view, their own subjective experience. And that is always a different experience compared to the other person's subjective experience.

The people in question need to find solutions coming from their own perspective, their own fundament that they have built through their own experience. And so you all need to be careful when you try to advise others. Try to listen to the Higher Self speaking instead of the lower part which lives in constant fear.

And you who are seeking advice, please do not take the words of another as being your own, because this will keep you locked in the victim stance where you have given your power away. You may take such words as a pointer, but please do not let others choose for you. Choose yourself what is best for you, and above all, always choose what your own intuition tells you.

Speaking of predictions as such, they are not a mystery or an enigma, and it is not a question of superstition. No, they are in fact an answer from the intelligence of science, because everything in existence has living consciousness. It is the same for the cards, or to be more correct, the symbols, numbers and colours which make up the different cards. For the colours then represent your feelings, and as they are put into symbolic form you are able to communicate with the cards through the overall field of conscious living intelligence, called the quantum field.

The quantum field, in which everything in physical manifestation exists and of which it consists, is a living mass of interchanging particles and waves, thought and matter. Thereby, through your own energy field, you are able to connect with the quantum entities making up the Tarot cards and their field. Your energy directed through the quantum field in a way envelops the cards used for predictions, and you then subconsciously direct the cards to move into an expression of your higher knowledge which is subconsciously keeping track of your unfolding life plan.

This quantum field then monitors the cards, and the energy pull from you will direct the person handling the deck of cards. The knowledge of your future, coming from yourself, will then express itself by directing and placing the cards into their specific consecutive order, showing the situation through the symbols and numbers on the cards.

This picture is however made available especially for the person who interprets the cards, and may vary from reader to reader dependent on their understanding, or their interpretation of the symbols on the cards.

These days more and more people are seeking self knowledge through the deck of Tarot cards, and, used this way, it is a tool of self realisation for all who feel drawn to it.

Incidentally, the way events happen in time is in fact similar to a deck of cards, as the future is not laid out in a linear and horizontal fashion. It is actually happening vertically and consists of lots and lots of 'slides' put on top of each other, which you get to load into the projector and organise along the way.

It may also be compared to running a film, a movie, consisting of a stream of pictures which describe the different scenes that make up the story. And when you look at every moment as one independent little picture, you can see that it is possible to interchange the scenes and make it into a different story, and thereby have a different future.

This is how it works. You have all these scenes which make up the present story of your movie. But then you may interchange scenes. Sometimes you are cutting them out and throwing them away to make new ones, or perhaps you are changing actors. And as you change the script as you go along, you change the very events that are being monitored. Finally, you may make another ending to the movie and make this one your final choice, instead of the previous one which you have decided you no longer like.

You are indeed yourselves the directors of your own life movies, and your collective choices make up your common world experience, widely screened.

Although you have other actors and you shoot your film on different locations, you yourself are the director, and you are deciding at every moment how this movie is manifesting itself. But you will not be able to see the result, the finished movie, until you end your life on earth. By the way, I got some help on this one from my darling 'twin partner', who wants to get back into business, he says...

Now, since time itself goes in loops, more or less like a roller coaster, it is understandable that you can only see part of the picture at any given point. And what concerns channels or psychics, fortune tellers and clairvoyants, is that they can only see, let's say, along their own 'waves' of energy, corresponding to their level of spiritual development. They have a sort of 'frequency range' open to them where they can view their specific 'network programs' from the 'station' they are connected to and get pictures transferred onto their inner screens. The 'stations' I am here referring to are certain celestial beings, guides, or also space stations that may be monitoring the information.

You can compare it to a television that is pre-set to receive only certain stations, let's say, only a couple of stations sending along their specific band of energy frequency. No living being has yet become a fully developed model of 'tell vision', but some may have a 'set vision' still in development.

Or let's say that the brain capacity is still in the development stage, and therefore one can only operate within a certain limited range of frequencies. And different channels have different frequencies, so you may get a different picture giving you different answers, and you may become upset or very confused because of this.

But then, know that it just looks different from different angles and different locations, stations, or view-points, so that you cannot get the whole picture all at once, and this of course is something you are not supposed to, either. Then the story behind the whole movie of the world would be disclosed prematurely, and you would not be able to enjoy finishing it. You would then understand the plot and altogether probably choose to get out of the action. 'Game over', as they say in the world of computer-games.

Then you would reach enlightenment and move through the time border and choose to go through to the light, without finishing and tying up all the loose ends. However, you need to make an ending that opens for a 'successor', in order to continue the evolution into the next stage, next octave of life on earth.

It's yours to consider, do you want to make it a movie with a happy ending or does it turn into a horror movie? Which may happen, if you do not collectively decide to go for the romance instead of continuing in violence.

What happens, in fact, when you surpass the speed of light, is that some of you will go to a higher octave of reality. Indeed, you will begin to measure universal time in octaves, because the octaves, consisting of seven inter-dependable proceeding steps, will be like borders to higher and higher experience and the evolution of your own dimensional brain capacity. It will accompany your love capacity and the new possibilities of creation within this sphere that you call reality on earth.

Some of you will be able to go through to another higher pitched octave, and maybe choose not to return. However, you will be taking your physical body with you, changed by an act of transformation from particles into waves only. But if you choose this route, you will be able to go back and teach your brothers and sisters who are left behind in the lower perception of reality. This would indeed be very beneficial, as you will then be able to come back, carrying with you the higher knowledge that you have acquired on this trip. This particular procedure of transformation from a physical body into a light body may be known under the term 'Ascension'.

This actually implies that you may be able to travel towards your future and get new understanding from your future, which you can bring back with you and use in the here and now. This is however only possible within the parameters of the divine law and order, and the principle that governs time.

However, you should know that your time is not up yet. And you get enough, let's say, possibilities from the knowledge of your heart to achieve the changes that you want to make. You should know too that the prophecies that have been made, for instance, by the medieval mystic called Nostradamus were indeed done within the understanding of time. At the present he is truly very happy to see that you hopefully will change your future so that his last predictions will not come into reality at all.

The process of a successful prophet is in fact to be proved wrong in the future, meaning that he then has done his job in such a manner that you yourself are looking ahead and changing a future filled with pain. Then you have listened to the positive aspect of the warnings given, and changed the future from being the result of your unconscious thoughts and feelings to become a future of your conscious choice. Make it a conscious choice of love, peace and harmony.

Now I would like to relay a message regarding the funds that are being set up in my name, in my memory, holding the money that is so graciously given and collected. I would like this money to be spent on spiritual education: given as scholarships to students of limited means and of all ages; to those who are seeking spiritual understanding, spiritual knowledge through an education in this field, in these alternative areas; and possibly to build, or set up centres for spiritual education. All in all, spend the money for the purpose of getting people to become able to help themselves, and help others through self-help.

I want to become a spiritual leader whose intention it is to help people become independent, and let them do this themselves through their own process. Because this is how you gain self-confidence, this is how you can start to feel worthy in your own eyes. Indeed I would like to see all the people of earth worthy of love, worthy of the love of themselves and of the Creator, and the love of each other.

This is my spiritual goal if I ever have one. This is the purpose that I would like to manifest on earth in my name. Because this way I see the possibility to spread the understanding of universal love consciousness, the divine consciousness of love. And give also, let's say, the average or 'poor' people the possibility of seeking alternative, spiritual education, so that lack of school money will not be an obstacle to their paths.

In the spiritual centres that you may set up, you can pay the fees of the teachers, the healers and the therapists, and so let people come in and get treatment or education, nearly without paying. And start helping them to develop their own abilities for healing through activating their own self-healing powers. Then they too are able to relay this power on to others by resonance.

This way you will start to take care of each other through self-help, and not through dependency. For any kind of treatment that encourages a dependency on a continuous chain of treatments is not helping in the long run. Everybody needs to choose to start healing him or herself from within, and what others can do is just to ignite this process of self-healing within the other.

Of course this doesn't mean that you should not collect money in order to help people that are starving not only for knowledge but for food. You need to help each other, and there is enough money and means in the world to distribute the help from the rich countries to the underdeveloped nations. But this is a subject for the governments and politicians, and not for me at this point. The same goes for any causes that deal with military aid. You need to sort this out yourselves, and my contribution at this time is to help you learn how to do this through your spiritual awakening.

I would like then to contribute to, or pay for, the education of spiritual teachers to teach students who have aspirations and talents to pass on the knowledge and go into the school systems. Go into educational systems with this knowledge and spread it further, so that you really will study to become enlightened, not through some outer force but directly from the source within.

You are to get the knowledge from the source which is your own divine consciousness, because this is the divine plan for humanity. That you yourself, by your own free will, turn inwards and recognise the presence of the light of the divine, and evolve through this self-realisation and by helping each other. So that those going at the front will turn around and pull the other ones up. And thereby you will make a chain of love, a circle of love around the whole world, that will transform and transmute the earth itself.

Because you all together comprise the consciousness of earth, and as you realise the potential of light within yourself, the earth itself will light up and become a star, the most beautiful source of light in this part of the universe. Then The Christ will have returned to you all, as he promised, and his work in this part of the universe will be accomplished.

All of you, the whole humanity, will become like sparkling diamonds on the top surface, in the crown of this star. Because you will be lit up from within. Your colours will make vibrations of the most beautiful music throughout the universe, and you will be honoured and recognised for who you are. The courageous children of space ship earth, who are bringing the gift of love through your free will in order to share it with the brothers and sisters from the worlds that you left. The worlds of the stars that shine their lights towards you as you are looking into the night sky.

Now you will yourselves become a star, and indeed the earthstar will be a superstar, a star of 'supra light' itself. And The Divine Creator will have recognised him and her self as the creation of light.

# Part 3

## *Personal and Global Responsibility*

# Chapter 11

How are you doing? I hope you are still with me, that you are still hanging in there. Then you are just my kind of type, courageous and curious and determined to go all the way, to see it through and this is all I ask for. That you read the book through, no matter how much you are able to understand or comprehend at first glance. But when you read what I have written word by word, at least some of it will glue to your thoughts.

Bear in mind that this book is written on several levels of understanding. It is written in fact on all seven of the levels that I have explained to you. The first level is obvious; it is the texture of the book that you are holding. The second level or dimension is the written page itself. The third level is what you understand as you read from sentence to sentence. The fourth level is what you comprehend as you lose track of time while reading.

The fifth level is the connection through love that you get as you are reading and relate it to your own life. It might also be sadness and tears, anger or disagreement, or whatever kind of emotions it awakens in you. The sixth level is the level where you touch my feelings, where you are able to connect with me and feel the underlying current of energy in the book, in between the lines.

And the seventh level is actually hidden from you. It is the text within the text, the deeper acknowledgement of the meaning, which you need to discover for yourself as you connect some of the words and link them together. It shouldn't be too hard. It becomes indeed a deeper level of understanding as you remember and transmit the knowledge through to your DNA. And this deeper meaning will give you insight, the insight of oneness, of the seventh dimension of yourself.

This book is also connected to all of your 7 chakras or emotional feeling centres which are placed from the bottom of your spine up through your body along the spine, ending on top of your head. I will give you a quick explanation because this is important to part of the understanding that I will deliver later.

As I have said, the chakras are centres of energy, which means that they do not exist as something physical in your body. However, they run straight through the different bodies, connecting them and functioning as transformers of energy. Even though science cannot detect them on the physical level, you can in fact feel them physically within your body.

The first chakra, called the root chakra, is the emotional centre where you relate to feeling safe in the world, safe within your own being and in the connection to your own parents, especially to your mother. And it also relates you to mother earth because it is the centre that holds your connection to earth. It is placed at the bottom tip of your spine.

The connection from the first chakra to the heart relates to the well being of your life on earth in its entirety, and whether you are feeling safe and happy about this fact.

The second feeling centre is called the sexual chakra, and it is obviously the emotional centre for sexual feelings, the sexual connection between the two sexes or the gender that you are attracted to. And as such it is also connected to your creativity and to the communication of creativity, within yourself as well as to the outside world, and the 'life lust', the joy of being alive, centred also through to the heart. It is placed approximately one inch below your navel.

The third chakra is the solar plexus chakra. It is connected to your outer expression and this is where you connect in the moment and feel the impact of other people's emotions on you. You are especially sensitive to the fear of rejection which you project from the two lower centres. The third chakra is also the emotional centre where you keep control over your feelings, where you either shut down your feelings or open yourself towards others. So it shows you how you express your life, and this expression is often due to the condition of the two lower chakras. It is centred within your guts, in the middle stomach area, and resembles the 'gut feeling'.

The fourth chakra is the heart chakra. It is placed within the middle of your chest, or actually exactly where you feel your heart.

That is, of course, the emotional centre for love. The feeling of earthly love, or love between two people, and love for your family as such. Ideally, this centre is to be the governing and balancing middle point in relation to all the chakras and their individual functions in your body and being.

Then there is the fifth chakra, which is the throat chakra. However, in-between the throat and the heart there is also an additional emotional centre developing. And it will develop as the fifth chakra to the degree that you express yourselves more and more as a global group. Because this is the universal love or heart chakra which connects you to humanity, to the love for humanity and the love for yourselves as human beings, as well as love for The Creator. However, I will just mention the fifth chakra as the throat chakra at this point.

Let me just go back and mention the connection between the solar plexus and heart chakras, which is the step that you are going to make in this next transformation phase. You are going to raise your emotional awareness, which is the same as your centredness, from being self-centred in the solar plexus, motivated by fear, to become heart-centred, focused in the fourth chakra which is motivated by love.

In the fifth chakra, the throat chakra, located at the bottom of your throat, you have the oral expression of your inner truth, of your wisdom expressed through language or through sound. And this is also connected with music, for the musicians who play an instrument with vocal accompaniment. The fifth chakra is also connected to the second chakra, which includes artistic expression. And so these two centres come together towards the heart as your artistic expression of love.

The sixth chakra is placed in your forehead, just in-between and above your eyebrows. This area is the so-called third eye. Here is your inner vision, or clairvoyance. It is connected to the pineal gland within the head and it forms a triangle, an inner screen, where you can start to get flashes of images. This may confuse you at first, since you don't actually see them with physical eyes, although they may seem just as clear to you.

But you should understand that it is like a projector in your head, a screen which is presently covered but will be lighted up as you grow in understanding. And then this sixth centre is connected to the heart. As you open up for love, you open up this inner vision and start to see the higher levels of existence, and you can see the different energy bodies.

You begin to see energy and you also start to see those who are surrounding you as your guides; those worlds that are presently hidden from your physical eyes are showing up too. Understand though that the physical eyes are not windows which take in the real world which you think you are seeing. They only ever take in what you allow yourself to see.

However, what is hidden is also being transmitted to the third eye, although that is physically closed. With practice, you can see much more of the unseen by using your third eye. What you see will be much more than you presently see with your physical eyes open.

In the seventh chakra you have the connection towards the divine, towards your Higher Self. It is placed on the top of your head, and in the understanding of eastern wisdom it opens towards the light from above like a lotus flower. This is the crown chakra. This is the crown that I have mentioned that you are all wearing, the crown that will arise and open up and reconnect you to the throne of your true being.

When this connection is made through to the heart, you will have total security within yourself, and you will have the knowledge of that which you really are in connection with your Higher Self.

As you understand already, the heart is the centre of the body because it is the centre for all your different emotional centres. Because, the important thing is that you equalise all the different feeling centres so that there is balance throughout your body. Work on getting emotionally balanced in all areas of your life. This is again connected to these chakras and the explanation that I have just given.

For this is the purpose of healing: when you receive healing, you receive the energy through the different chakras, and because the heart is increasingly taking over as the manager of your emotions and your body, it is going to be possible more and more often to get an instant balancing. And that means that your own heart will give you healing.

Up until now you have been centred through your solar plexus centre. Therefore you have been unbalanced because the expressions of your centre have derived from the impressions coming from the outside world. You have balanced yourself from the imbalance of others outside of you, instead of from your inner force of love in your heart. You have been taking the energies from others as fuel for your own body, instead of getting your engine running in the heart to produce love for yourself.

Now, the reason I am explaining these subjects so thoroughly is that I want to make a connection between love and technology. What I would really like you to start studying is precisely the technology of love, because the technology of love is running the whole universe.

It is also running the mechanical technology. But, the mechanical technology is what you have created outside of yourselves in order to get to know what is going on inside. You cannot see this as long as you have closed your third eye, your inner vision. But as you start on your path towards inner knowledge, you will at last understand the principle which is used for technology on the outside, in the material world.

You will find the same principle applied in the technology for computers as in the technology for all kinds of gadgets that you use in your daily appliances. It is the same formula that the engines of your selves are using for their daily operations within your body. Because the inside is equal to the outside, and you express through your daily lives what you have hidden from yourself in the subconscious.

However, it may not be within the twinkling of an eye that you realise what the connections are, though in principle they are obvious. But the understanding needs to come through your own self-realisation.

First, you must be willing to see what you are creating, and take the full responsibility for your life by acknowledging that you yourself are the creator behind your creation, that in fact you are both the creator and the creation at the same time. This means that your life truly belongs to you, and that you are responsible for making whatever you want out of it. At any time, any moment of your life.

The technology of emotions, of love, of compassion also runs through the scientific world. Because it is interacting with thoughts, it is causing expectations when you run experiments, for instance, in physics or mathematics or in whatever area you are conducting your experimentation.

Because you see, you are directing the outcome of your experiments through your expectations, or through your presumed expectations. When you are looking for reasons for cancer for instance, you will find certain connections that will delude you into thinking that you have discovered the cause of the cancer itself.

However, it is only a component, a symptom along with a whole group of other components present, and those may vary from person to person or from sickness to sickness. You need to think in terms of holistic thinking and find the emotional reasons behind the physical symptoms.

You need to be aware of this fact so that you don't place your trust, for instance, in experiments made by the manufacturers of potentially harmful drugs and chemical medication. And so it is important for you to understand that this also means that you, and you alone, are able to treat yourself just by your changing your own beliefs, by your own redirecting of your thoughts, by self-healing.

If you learn how to perform healing on others, you also learn the principles of self-healing. And this is what you are all requested to do within yourselves. Because the cells of your body are at all times programmed by your thoughts, beliefs and emotions, and you need to increase your self esteem in order to increase the immune defence system throughout your body. And this is the first step towards total balance.

You need to recover the balance in all areas of your life, especially the balance between work and play, or to have joy at work. Because you can no longer keep on doing a job that is not fulfilling you, that is not giving you pleasure, because that will in turn damage your internal systems and your body, through your emotional signals.

You need to start loving what you do, and doing what you love. And as a result you will indeed start doing what you are pre-programmed for. Your internal message centre has been trying to tell you not to suffer through pain, but to start to express yourself through your own wishes; to do what you really and truly feel like doing; and only your heart can tell you what this is. And thereby you are being led towards a future where you let your heart decide your own destiny.

Now then, this is not going to be a textbook to explain the energy-flow of the body, or the chakras or the functions of the body. But, I need to explain some of these things in connection with my next statement. And that statement is as follows; "You do not live in your bodies." Hardly any of you live in your bodies, even if you think you do.

First of all, only a tiny little part of yourself is able to take, or let's say to get, enough space within your body; and second, your understanding and your feelings and your abilities were not meant to be confined within the body to start with. However, as you live on the physical level, it is important that you begin to live in your physical bodies.

By that, I mean that in order to feel comfortable with yourself, you need to start truly feeling happy with your physical appearance. Begin to find the happiness of being in the body, but keeping the knowledge of the infinite soul. With the access to the infinite soul, you can start to enjoy being bodily incarnated. Because you can finally begin to feel whole and safe as you are reconnected towards home.

Now, what I mean by not living in your body is that you, your consciousness, your thoughts, your memory, are not living inside the body itself. They are resonating in the body, yes. They have a magnetic attraction to the body, yes. But that doesn't mean that you are your body, or let's say, live a 'bodily' life.

Because, your very memory is not situated in your brain tissue, and all that you are experiencing throughout your days, which you think you are storing in the memory somewhere in the brain itself, is not being kept in the brain at all. No wonder that your scientists cannot find the physical location of any memory. Indeed, they are pondering about what happens when a person is still able to remember things, although his brain was severely damaged in an accident.

Your historic memory is stored in the grid surrounding the earth, in the Akashic Records. And the function of the brain is to resonate as your personal code when accessing this grid. You store away your acquired knowledge for future use, let's say for eternal safekeeping, because you don't need to have it all available all the time. It is similar to storing away written information on floppy disk files in your desktop computer.

The function of the brain is the same as that of a big parabolic antenna. The liquid that is floating in the brain is a resonating fluid, and the neurones that are components of the brain are small antennae that connect with the part of you that has its position in the grid, connected to your time and place of birth.

They resonate with your experience of an event, and thereby you get your own personal memory of what may be, let's say, a world event. (Just look at the connection between the words 'reason' or thinking, and 'resonate'.)

This is one of the reasons why you all experience the same events so totally differently, even down to events within your family.

You remember them differently because you respond differently, because you have a brain uniquely composed of your own individual emotional codes, and of your previous positions in the grid as well, based on the soul evolution that you are undertaking.

As I have said, you are not truly living in your body, but in the field surrounding the body. Part of the memory is also resonating within the auric field; however, that is mostly the information that you do not need to store, as it is your daily consciousness.

Your sub-consciousness, however, is stored within your skin, within the physical components of the biological body skin, as the emotional impulses of physical memory. And this is why your body gets sick, ill, diseased, when you have experienced something which is painful emotionally. Because the reaction to the event gets stored in your physical body. It is the impressions which get stored, not the mental memory of the event itself but the emotional response.

Your emotional state of being as you experienced the event will store itself within your biological body as a subconscious emotional memory. And this is what you need to heal when you start to work on clearing your patterns from the past. You need to reconnect with your emotional memory within your body, as well as with the memories of the event, perhaps many lifetimes ago, stored in the Akashic Records. This way you heal the reason for your body being in dis-ease, in order to rebalance yourself.

Now, the reason I said that you are not living in your body goes along with the fact that you are aware of this. As many of you are kind of just floating around, existing in the surroundings of your own life, because you do not feel good about your own body. But you would be much better off if you learned to reconnect, and really went inside instead of experiencing your life on the outside, in the surrounding field, trying to peek in while you are walking there beside yourself.

When you get inside your body you get access to all there is, and also the fear and pain that you are trying to escape from. But the harder you try to escape, the more painful it gets, because whatever you give energy to builds the very energy charge that will reflect itself back at you. So, instead of escaping the body because you or someone else has judged it to be unattractive, sinful, too fat or too thin, you can start to reaffirm your own creation with love.

By focusing on all kinds of faults and sicknesses that you are unable to love, you are forever separated and left on the outside. This is indeed the situation where you need to go within and heal your judgement. You do this by practising your breathing.

By breathing deeply, all the way down to your belly, you are breathing yourself into the centre of your being. And you will start to feel that you reconnect inside of your body. Because actually, for most of you, breathing is shallow and just on the surface, and this also reflects your state of mind, which is that of fear.

In other words, you cannot really dispense with, let's say, meditation in the sense of breathing, or mindfulness to your own existence, the breath of life, your life energy, for shorter or longer periods at a time. And you will also notice how much more pleasure you will get within your body when you start to meet what, or who, is actually there.

Nothing on the inside is alien and unknown. The truth is that you know everything that is going on within the body at all times, except that you do not want to acknowledge your own responsibility for it. Because you have a tremendous fear of your self; maybe because you think that your emotions are too powerful for you to handle. And this is because of the impact of those previous events, which you are hiding skin deep, in the subconscious.

But you can start little by little to lift that lid, with gentle therapeutic assistance. You are not meant to do it all by yourself, you know; it would go so much faster and easier if you open up for others to help you. And if you do, you will also create work amongst yourselves, because many of you want to work with people instead of machines or doing paperwork.

Begin to work within yourselves instead of working on the outside. Work doing something creative like artwork, and thereby make something that will help you and others to heal themselves. Art itself is a form of therapy or healing, as it is the expression, or recognition, of the present inner state of being.

An artist certainly shows off his or her soul through their work of expression, and they are therefore able to give resonance to their fellow human beings. There is a great demand for art in your world - especially for the art that you can make for yourself. This would have the greatest effect on you, as each and every one of you are yourselves creators.

Again, remember that the colours in artwork, like those in a painting, will respond to your thinking, creative thoughts, and that music will respond to your emotions. So the connection between music and painting is truly most effective.

Your awareness is not confined within the physical body. Your awareness is available everywhere, however, it makes a focus in the third dimension through the body. And in order to be able to really start living and wake up from the dream that you are dreaming is your life, you need to feel safe enough to stay in the body for any amount of time.

You can start to experience with all your senses, both physical and emotional, and not only during the times of making love, for instance. It could be a great help to get yourselves massage therapy or some other types of body-related treatment which can make you feel comfortable physically.

There is another thing. Please do not take yourselves so incredibly seriously. Instead, you can try to play your way through life. Play, because there is indeed a higher game at work, and you have the freedom to improvise all the way instead of thinking that you have to follow a path predestined for you. Certain of the main posts along this path are decided beforehand, yes, and thereby you have some directions to follow, but otherwise you are free to improvise.

The energies will follow your demands and always show up as manifestations of your intent. And this means that you can be flexible and ought to be flexible, because in that way you will experience and learn, and gain the most as you go along.

When I say that you do not have your awareness within your body, it is because awareness is also connected to the feeling centres, the chakra system. Each of the seven chakras mentioned above corresponds to the appropriate dimension, so that the first chakra corresponds to the first dimension, the second chakra to the second, and the third to the third and so on.

This also means that the energy-bodies, which make up the auric field, also correspond one by one to the different dimensions. So you have a part of yourself in all levels or dimensions, a part of yourself that is aware of what is going on in all dimensions simultaneously. This means that you are truly a multidimensional being, that you have the capacity to be all over and everywhere at the same place.

In fact, you are the All Encompassing Creator yourself, as you create on all levels simultaneously. You are the creation that you, the creator, have manifested on all levels at the same point in time. So understand this when I am now going to tell you the answer to the question of whom you are, and why you are here.

The answer is indeed that you are a God, a creator, one part of The One Infinite Creator, and you are his/her creation at the same time.

So acknowledge this fact within your heart, acknowledge what you are, that you exist in order to know who you are, to see how you are. For The Creator is all and nothing at the same time.

He, the Creator, was nothing until he became everything, or She, the Creator, was no-body until she became every-body.

So understand that the all and the nothingness are one and the same, but it wouldn't know the difference unless it created itself and thereby became The Creator as You.

When you do your part, when you take full responsibility and care for yourself, then you have done sufficient. And as all of you do the same, you are expressing your selves to the fullest, showing the inner potential. As you change yourself, you change your world, because the earth itself and you are interconnected through the pulse of the 'heartbeat' in the earth. This is the electromagnetic pulse of the gravity of the earth fields.

They are connected to the frequency of the human heart/brain rhythm, so that the heartbeats make the earth resonate, and thereby you create the weather patterns which express the emotional conditions of humanity. So you create the development which takes place both within and on the surface of the earth's crust, all together as a unit.

As each and everyone has an impact on this planet, so each and everyone also has an impact on each other, and as a whole you have impact on each and everything.

So you are all in it together. You are responsible to yourselves, to earth and to humanity itself. And in turn you are responsible to this galactic system, this universe, and this universe in turn is responsible to the 'Time Lords' of the universes, and they again are responsible to the even higher universe of universes. So it goes on and on. This universe is a cell within the body of a greater universe, which is a cell within an even greater being, and so on. And there is infinity within infinity within infinity, towards infinity.

And your world is thereby reflecting a higher world, a higher reality. The beauty of your world is but a faint reflection of the beauty of the beauty of the higher dimension. And when you see an especially beautiful work of art for instance, it just may be reminding you of an inner beauty that you know exists within your inner vision, and so you know that you have recognised a higher part of yourself.

So please go on and recreate beauty, create with feeling, create with sound, and understand that as you learn to 'tune in' to the inner universe, you will learn to perfect the sound of the A-tone, because it is the basic musical note of creation. And you will start to harmonise through the sound of the pure A. Which is also, by no coincidence of course, the first letter of your alphabet.

Harmonise yourselves through the healing of the colour of A as well, and thereby you will rise like a rocket towards your next destination. The destination itself is unknown, but because it is within, it is known in the unknown. Just as I myself am known as Diana; however, I am totally unknown; or tell me what you think, is this how you knew me?

Now, it is the same with you, you think that you know yourself from the perceived levels of your physical expression, but truly you are something totally different. You are total love, total wisdom and total resurrection.

Know that you will go through the same procedure when you are ready. You will lift your spirits, you will literally lift your spirit, and this you may even be able to do from within your physical body. You can become able to transform the body from one level to the next without going through physical death and thereby you can experience the shift into love technology. A shift made through the technology of compassion.

# Chapter 12

Allow me to elaborate somewhat further on the subject of love and the technology of love. First, we have to establish that love is an energy charge that emanates from sound/light as an expression of the creator. And this expression is the foundation of all of the creation. It is the charge that is bringing evolution throughout the creation; the energy charge of knowing, of The Creator knowing itself through love.

The Creator is all encompassing, and is the light and the darkness at the same time. And in order to know The Creator, you create both darkness and light in your life. Perhaps not always at the same time, and perhaps you change between light or happiness, and darkness or unhappiness, which are the energies of positive and negative experiences. However, the point is that you should know yourself through love whether it is in darkness or in light, and stop placing judgements on either of the experiences.

For if you judge your experience, you are not experiencing the love, you are experiencing instead the thought energy of the event unfolding. You probably know, from your own experience of moments of bliss and happiness, that if you think the thought, "Now I am happy, yes, this is what happiness is all about," the happiness seems to vanish in an instant. And, of course, this is due to the judgement which you passed on the situation.

In order to be happy, in order to stay within the experience and feeling of happiness, you need to leave judgement behind. You need to allow to happen just what you are experiencing, without judgement. For judgement is the absence of love. Judgement chases away the energy charge of All Encompassing Flow in order to put the experience in one of the boxes that you can mentally label, perhaps as happiness; not as the feeling of happiness, but as the thought of what happiness is.

What you are really seeking is to experience happiness without needing to judge it as such, as happiness or bliss, but to allow the feeling of the experience just to be in the moment. And that moment may thereby expand, and you will stay within the feeling for any length of time. This is what is going to happen to you in the 'no-time' experience. Then you will stop judging and rise above, and so come into the zone of 'zero point' time.

Bear in mind that the forces of darkness are equally important to you as are the forces of light present on earth. Because without the charge between them, without the possibility of creation that exists as friction between the two polarities, you would not have the possibility of creating anything new, and therefore of knowing the creation as The Creator.

For me, it is important to get you to understand that if you stop your tendency to compare your experiences, whether to the experiences of others, to your pre-set wishes or to your expectations, you will finally start to find peace within yourself. Instead of making comparisons, start to experience perfection in the perceived imperfections of your life.

In order to make it a peaceful world, you need to find peace within your own existence, within your own personal world, and thereby manifest the expression of peace on a larger scale amongst you. For it is judgements which have caused wars to start from within you, moral judgements and your judgement between opposing opinions, turned into self-righteousness.

As you judge another you certainly also judge yourself, and so this dispute can never come to an end. You argue from your own point of view and refuse to put yourself in the other person's or country's position. You must understand that the negotiation has to start from within yourself. And the willingness to allow imperfection has to show itself within your own life, as you stop judging your life and your position in it based on its outer reflections, that is on the level of success and approval that you have at the present time.

When you judge yourself, you project judgement on your surroundings, and when you start to make comparisons, it can never become a perfect world for both the sides compared. But the world is perfect with its imperfections, because in imperfection it allows you to find compassion and become compassionate towards that which is not perfect, or that which you perceive as not perfect. And thereby you have created a world that is teaching you about compassion. And this is the second path on which you will start to embark as you discard the old path of judgement.

Many of you are fearful of the predictions carried in the biblical text called 'The Revelation' which foretells the coming of an antichrist, expressed as the number 666. However, I will now give you my interpretation, for you to ponder and decipher for yourself. Because in fact it is a personal coding and you are asked to respond to your own inner truth in this as in everything else.

The numbers 666 are a distortion, truly their opposite, which turned around is 999. And 999 are the numbers preparing for completion. The completion occurs as you add one, or oneness, to 999 and you get a 1,000, a new year thousand.

This is what the prediction is all about. The new year thousand which is giving you the possibility of experiencing love on earth, an experience which is granted as you go through the procedure of making your choices, on an individual as well as a larger scale.

The distortion of the 999 shows you that there are forces in the outside world that will try to stop you from turning around, from changing your point of view and changing your perception. Instead, those forces want to hold you in chains, hold you at a lower point of understanding and evolution.

This symbol may also be seen as a sequence of musical notes. If you view 666 as symbols in terms of musical notes, they are placed on the lower scale of a music line and it is obvious that when you turn them around to show 999, they will express musical notes on the higher scale. They resemble the notes of the higher scale of evolution, of your possibilities in a higher octave.

So it is the distortion of your fulfilment that you will need to guard against. Look out for those that will try to keep you down, that will block you from reaching your full potential, from reaching up to your higher consciousness, and keep you in ignorance on the lower level of existence. There are forces in your world that actually send out sound vibrations on a lower scale, and this lower scale is also emanating the 666 idea.

These are low frequency sound waves; waves with lower vibrations which send out patterns to distort the higher vibrations of love. However, it is not possible to stop the higher vibrations of love. But it is possible to send out distortions which will then try to keep you in confusion, keep you in fear and doubt instead of reaching up and asking for your higher truth and your Higher Self to emerge.

The illusion of separation is the pathway on which you have walked on the lower scale. But as you reach up to find the second path, you will meet the truth, which is that you have never been separated to start with. However, the main importance has been placed on the distortion of your mind , because the dominance of the masculine principle has been prevalent in your society, in your world, for the last thousands of years.

This has indeed confused you because you have been living with a double morality and thereby denying the second part of yourself, which is your intuitive ability to create through the feminine principle, and feel the ability of love. Due to this fact you now have a tendency to think love instead of feeling love.

You have adopted all kinds of thought biases that tell you what love is supposed to be, how love is supposed to be expressed and how a perfect relationship should be; as well as placing such importance on your outside looks and an emphasis on the perceived level of success in life, and how you judge success within your own self.

The truth is that there is actually only one true feeling, and that is the feeling, the sensation, the experience of love. Everything else that you think you feel is emotion. And the emotions are the results of thoughts that diversify and distort the feeling because of judgement. In judgement you sabotage the real feeling of the feeling as you start thinking the feeling instead of experiencing it.

Then, in order to get in tune with yourself, you need to allow the sound of love, the light of love to penetrate. Just allow the sensation of sound and light to become the vibration in your body. Because this vibration is vibrating as love, you are thereby becoming the love that you are seeking within you, as yourself.

In ending judgement, you will allow for wholeness to enter, and you will end separation because the thought of judgement is the separation itself. You separate yourself by judging yourself as being separate from the experience of the very experience which you experience. Instead you are to allow yourself to become the experience of love itself.

Then you can see that you yourself are the force behind the lower vibrations that are blocking your own rise in consciousness, this force which is emanating the 666. Because you see, as you judge your own love, your own ability to love, you become your own fear, and your own fear is trying to stop you from experiencing the love that you seek.

So look inside yourself for the 'beast', or your dark side. Look for your shadow thoughts which are telling you that you are not worthy of love, that you need to continue to experience fear, because fear is all that you know.

Stop these thoughts by allowing the feeling of love to emanate and bring light into all the frightened spots within your self, in your body, in your mind and the repressed consciousness of your being. And thereby you are going to turn the outside technology inside, and you yourself become the instrument behind the inner technology.

You will yourself apply the remedies that heal you from the inside. Because as you allow love to come in and fill up and take the place of your doubt and fear, you will create the immune defence from within and begin recharging yourself from the inside, and start to give new orders to your cells and the organs of your body.

These will be orders made in complete trust and knowledge of your own worthiness, and so you will give yourself the benefit of becoming a compassionate God to your own creation, your own body, your own being. And as you become the loving, compassionate Creator-god that you are seeking for yourself, then you will see this same image in the mirror of your fellow human beings, and your world will mirror it at large.

Know that the Second Coming of Christ is you. Your Christ Selves are coming into being as you allow the love and the light from within into your own consciousness. There is the same potential within every walking human being on earth as there was for Christ Jesus, for he was just coming to show you your own potential. You are all brothers and sisters in spirit, because you are all children of the same parent, the mother/father Creator of Love.

# ✳ Chapter 13

I have come to talk to you about how to open your heart. First of all, you need to realise that your hearts are being closed. But to realise that, you must know how it feels to have an open heart. To help you 'find' your heart, there are many spiritual workshops being held by different 'New Age' teachers on the physical plane, and they usually arrange them in the setting of a weekend workshop.

However, many of you may not feel drawn to these kinds of workshops, perhaps because you feel that they are too removed from your reality, or what you perceive as your reality. And perhaps there is too much focus on 'angelwork' and white clothing and ceremonies and so forth; and these are putting you off because they don't seem to fit into your sturdy environment.

Well, now I am here to talk about some other ways of following up this blockage to an open heart. Because, you understand that although some of you in previous lifetimes are the priests and priestesses from the ancient temples, you are not to live in temples now. You are not to go through the initiations and replay the ceremonies, because you have done all of this before and it now represents only the outer initiation.

The inner initiation goes on right here in your own life, in your own lifetime, because it is your very relationship to your self and to others. And your search, your pursuit of the passage which is the path to the inner self leads through the challenges that you meet in your everyday life, because the worst enemy of your heart is the fear of change. The fear of going into that which is unknown. And this fear makes your heart contract everyday.

It makes your heart fearful, which makes your feelings fearful. And this in turn makes you say 'no' to all the challenges about which your heart would have been happy in safer circumstances, happy for the opportunity to try out new things. Whereas feelings of love would have made you say 'yes' in order to pursue your continuous growth, and perhaps choose a new and more fulfilling direction in your life.

However, this is indeed your present challenge: to open yourself to the opportunities given in your everyday lives, opportunities that present themselves as unexpected invitations, as new possibilities which you may fear because you are afraid of becoming disappointed, of being judged and of being unable to cope.

Males are normally more comfortable with this type of challenge in their work situations, but they fear the challenge of pursuing their feelings. And females are more adventurous respecting the emotional challenge than they are in meeting the demands of pursuing a career for themselves.

But if you dare to go through and pursue new challenges as if you are just diving into unknown water, then your heart will soar, it will open up with the pleasure and satisfaction of taking that risk. Because the nature of the heart is one of expansion, of broadening out, of sharing of itself. The heart is not happy with a response that says, "No, thank you, I am too afraid." Your heart is only satisfied when it hears, "Yes, I will try," from the courageous you. And the heart would not see a 'no', or a rejection from others on the outside, as an attack on itself.

Your daily lives give you all the possibilities you need when you start to communicate from your hearts. But if you just keep your thoughts and your feelings to yourself, your heart is still contracting. However, if you dare to speak up, you are to speak about what is on your mind, what you have painfully hidden in your heart. Speak, preferably directly to the person towards whom you have directed your anger or disappointment, and tell this person of your feelings. Thereby you ease the burden of your heart, so that the energy from your contracted love can reopen and allow you to become honest, honest with yourself and honest with the other.

Know that if you are quarrelling, you are arguing because you are angry with yourself for posing as someone else. If you are throwing words of wrath and bitterness at the other person, you are receiving the same back, but in doing this you are also opening up for the possibility of love. You may not appreciate this at the time, but you can cultivate the ability to start recognising it so that you understand your anger as a door opener.

Your sudden outburst is a heart opener because in that moment you have the possibility of expanding and growing because you are in contact with your true feelings and emotions; you are daring to let out into the open what you have suppressed inside of yourself. And everything that you keep a lid on will stay under pressure until that pressure is eased. Otherwise you end up with bodily dis-ease.

So you need to communicate; you need also to accept the challenge of expressing your feelings when you are afraid of becoming hurt and rejected. But you do not need to speak in such a way that you hurt someone else in the process. You can speak in such a manner that you express everything from the point of view of your own feelings, how you are experiencing the situation, and therefore you do not need to make a frontal attack on the personality of your opponent.

Because you both have different opinions on the situation at issue, you know that both of you are probably in great fear of losing face, of being proved wrong. But you should know that the fear of being proved wrong is the ego's fear, the ego's fear of self-destruction. The goal of the ego is to keep itself posted in the lead position in your mind, guarding your own personal interest, because the ego is your outer measure of your inner expression towards the outside world.

Another thing, please start to become honest with your children, because your children are picking up all your signals all the time. They know when a lie is coming from your mouth because your body language and the tone of your voice shows them that you are speaking with a 'false tongue'.

By doing this, you give damaging signals to your children because they learn that they may also express themselves in this way. And they discover that they cannot trust your truth, because it is being called truth even when they know you are lying. So they become confused and lose faith both in you and in themselves.

When you open yourself up to the possibility of seeing your life as an ongoing initiation in spiritual realisation, you also open up for another level of living. You can start to really live your life fully by taking the opportunities that life is handing you, instead of steering away from everything that presents itself as change, challenge and disruption of your familiar routines.

When you live your daily routines, you put an automatic pilot in charge of steering your body. You do not really experience, you are just going through your daily experience as if sleep walking. Then, however, something may happen and disrupt you. You might be experiencing an accident or a great disappointment and in that sense you are being awakened against your will. But this is indeed an opportunity to be welcomed as it offers the possibility of starting a new life which is fully realised, instead of going on living in a passive dream.

You need to activate yourself and become an active participant in your own life. And this you do by choosing action. Choosing challenge; choosing the opportunity to grow in self-confidence by accepting the challenges; accepting them with courage even if they fill you with an uncomfortable excitement, with stage fright and all kinds of butterflies all over your body.

For those are the signs of being alive, of living in your body and not merely existing only in your heads. Feel the fear and then do it anyway. Your love for yourself will grow tremendously if you just allow yourself to try anything that you decide to do, in spite of your initial fears.

These are challenges for the upcoming years; to start experiencing fully, and fully experiencing. And you need not go through an extensive sequence of spiritual workshops just to be able to start seeing angels in your environment, or to experience that you are indeed living your life surrounded by angels – they are your fellow human beings.

Just know that the very people who give you the most trouble, the ones who pick fights with you, are in fact the people who love you the most. They are indeed the brothers and sisters of the heart who know of your need to learn and therefore make an agreement with you to teach you a lesson! So, you interchange lessons and get cross with each other, you quarrel and scream and you cry your hearts out, just to finally get to express some truth.

You will discover that all the while you are doing all of this for your own benefit, for your love of each other and for yourself, so that you can finally start realising how to open your hearts.

For in the middle of pain, in the middle of anger, there is this momentary peak where you can breathe deeply and turn inside. And from there you can trace your feelings and understand what are their real cause, what kind of hidden event is hiding behind the expressions of anger, of sadness, of bitterness or jealousy. In this manner you can return back to your feelings and talk to your inner child who is harbouring these painful imprints, and then in turn talk to the person who caused the feelings to occur in the first place, or to a therapist if the other person is not available.

In this way you can become aware of the suppressed feelings hidden deep inside you and open up your heart once more to the flow of love and harmony. You need to honour these feelings in order to be honest with yourself. This is the first and most important step towards the development of emotional freedom. Freedom to express what you are through what you feel and thereby take back your courage; the courage to experience your life with a heart expanding with love, instead of a heart constricted by fear.

All the physical angels surrounding you are souls that are going through their own development. Some of them have burdens on their wings so that they may not be all white and shiny, but appear in colours of different shades. Their wings may even have become dark, along with the once white gowns that they wear. But bear in mind that, as you go through your own cleansing process, you will realise that the dirt is just an illusion of the mind, as are the burdens, which are how sorrows appear.

As you cleanse yourself with honest insight, you will start to see the true beings with whom you are surrounding yourself; and indeed, throughout the world you are meeting yourself in different coloured expressions of the divine and the angelic.

For as you learn to recognise the inner shiny being, you understand that you are all worthy, you are all equal and made from the same source and you no longer need to judge and compare yourself to others and others to you. And you no longer need to fight against each other because this is just another fight against yourself.

You will start to recognise that what all the others are trying to show you is your own search for your inner self, and that when you find yourself, others will also find themselves in you.

Then there will be an inner shift arising from within, a shift in your DNA caused by a shift in the components of your genes, for the shift in consciousness will cause a rearrangement of the genes. Some of those genes that are presently switched on, those that are programming your fear, both your thoughts of fear and your feelings of fear, will be switched off. And those that are presently switched off due to lack of love will be turned back on, and you will be changed from within because of this mutation in the decoded components of your genes.

This will cause a change also in your immune system, so that in fact you will become resistant to some of the current diseases that you most fear, for instance the HIV virus. You can see this manifested even now in some parts of the world, for certain groups of people are already resistant because of their prevalent thoughts and beliefs. I am here referring to tests conducted on groups of Swedish people. But then you may object that they are just a privileged group, for it is true that they are groups of people who have not been touched to any great degree by this disease.

This has happened also because it was not their lot to experience the disease to start with, which indicates that their experiences might be of a different nature. You all have karmic issues to clear. Karmic issues are the cause and effect of situations from the past that are catching up with you. They illustrate your beliefs and your relationship to yourselves and your bodies.

In the case of AIDS, it reflects your relationship to your sexuality, especially the shame that you connect with sexuality, such as in homosexual relationships. But it also refers to the pain of people in underdeveloped countries who may not be expressing sex only as an act of love, but also express sex as a way of trading what they have to offer for what they want to get. Because of their lack of daily sustenance, they choose to trade the precious possession of their body and sexuality against hard currency.

Understand, when you finally change the world with compassion, you are going to change from within. You change the build-up of your own bodies, the make-up of your cells, and thereby renew your whole inner system. And this is made possible by a spontaneous mutation, and it is happening as I speak. A mutation caused by a change of perception, a change of perspective.

To your amazement you will witness that the human race will change from within, quite literally, since the change will commence from the DNA molecules. And although you may look the same on the outside, the Inner Light technology will rearrange the whole order of your body. Rearrange the whole system within the body so that you will become renewed as a different race, as multidimensional or love-dimensioned beings.

Stop looking around at your fellow human beings in the world as if they were your enemies out there to get you. The only one who is out there to get you is you yourself. Because you need to find yourself again, you need to address yourself in order to find you, the inner part of your self.

Understand that every human being living in your environment is a participant in the same game of life. They have ranged themselves along with you in order to start to open your eyes to the benevolence of the universe. Because the universe as The Creator, and the creation as The Creator, is providing you out of love with a physical playground where you run around and keep on hunting in the forests of thoughts and feelings until you find what you are seeking. And that is indeed the inner core of you, which is the ever-burning flame of the candle in the winds of life.

Understand that when you start to get this particular outlook from within your life, you will also get a new vision of the human beings with whom you surround yourself and of human beings all over the globe. And in response, the DNA will automatically start to rearrange itself throughout your body.

Within your body it will be reflected in a wondrous procedure of healing throughout your whole being. Each of you are to heal yourselves through this understanding of the divine nature of all and everything, and with this realisation you do not need to stay in duality any longer, but can move on and become oneness yourself.

Oneness is found when you are at one with your heart, when you are at one with your intuition, when your own needs and the needs of the creator of your heart are one and the same. Then you have embodied oneness and you move up to the next level of the expression of self.

 # Chapter 14

As I speak, the year 1997 is about to close. And this also marks the ending of this, my first book. However, after we have had an intermission, both you and I, we will meet again in the next book which already exists on the spiritual plane.

It is shining in front of me, white and beautiful, and you will meet me there again within yourself. As you open the book, you will also open up yourself. But until then we will wrap up the process in this book and leave it for you to integrate. Also, I will need to integrate and wrap up my previous life, the way it has been conducted, through my new understanding, through my new insight.

In this way I will be able to move on to a new start, the start of a New Year, a new future. And so it is with the earthly years. You go through cycles, commencing in the beginning of the year. You dance around the clock, starting out new and fresh. You dance around the seasons of the year and mark the different seasons within your minds and your feelings, as you do through the outer markings of winter, spring, summer and autumn.

Your life goes in cycles, and so do your lives on a larger scale, and so do the years within your life. So, as you realise that you are taking part all the time in the ever turning wheel of life, you are more and more able to appreciate unexpected turns of events and the unknown, which play their surprises upon you when you least expect it.

It needs to be this way, because otherwise you would be pre-programmed and become robots instead of creative human beings.

As your understanding progresses, you will perhaps come to believe that you need to give up much of your present life, much of your present comfortable condition and many of your achievements, in order to become 'spiritual'. But that is not quite so, not if you choose to do it the internal way.

For then you are going into your inner experience and will

experience the change within yourself instead of experiencing it through outer cataclysms. For you see, it is necessary to address all that which you have been taking for granted, everything, and that includes the manner in which you earn your salaries and wages.

Because, when you reflect upon yourself and, let's say, understand the smaller sacrifices that are necessary in order for you to become honest with yourself, then perhaps you can expect the larger corporations to do the same. Expect honesty from the powerful leaders of the corporations that are ruling the main part of the industries and your community, and which rule the world at large.

Understand that your world is indeed ruled by the power of money, and not any kind of money. It is ruled by the money of crime, the money of greed, of inside trading, the black currency hidden from your sight. And this, of course, is only possible because you all do the same. You all seek to hide your income and how you dispose of it from those around you.

In the core of your being you are not comfortable with showing yourself as you are, showing your self worth or lack of it. You do not even dare to show off everything you physically own because you live in fear of having it taken away from you. And as long as you are not willing to be visible, you cannot expect that society on the largest scale will be willing to give up its privileges and become visible to your scrutiny.

But all the secrecy and all the corruption is falling away due to its own dishonesty. Because the components that make up these systems are of course the singular people that are standing behind them, those in the top rank and downwards. And many of these people within the system are now feeling the pull from their soul, which is telling them to become honest and visible and make their position known, not only to themselves, but also to the world.

So, then you get all the scandals of the financial world, the scandals that are at present hitting home in the East, but this is like a global snowball that is rolling and rolling, and it will roll over a lot of banking corporations along its path. So you are bound to get a breakdown of the economic world system, and this could actually happen at any time. You need to be prepared however, because as this happens you are to rebuild on new ground, a new structure comprising an economic and geopolitical system that will sustain humanity as a whole, and not favour only those in the industrial countries.

In order to do this, you have to be willing to share what you have. And in doing so, you have to be safe enough to be willing to give up the need to defend yourself with weapons. You see, the cost of the present defence systems throughout the world in itself represents enough money to feed the whole population of the world on a daily basis.

In order for this to be anything else than an unrealised utopia, you have to attend to changing the consciousness of the world today.

Understand that if you stop fearing each other by your focus on theft and competition, or fearing lest the way you distribute your finances should become visible, then you may be willing to start anew with a fresh approach to building up a New World Federation of Unity. This will happen when you dare to start to be open and show yourselves at your true value. This is not the money that you keep to yourself, but the inner qualities of human love and compassion, for yourself as well as for humanity at large.

This New World Government based on Unity may be built upon a similar structure as that of the United States of America, which has a structure of a governmental umbrella that covers the independent 52 states representing the United States.

However, this is not exactly the plan that is presently in the works and which underlies the dispositions of the World Bank today. There are such plans for a new world order, but those in charge of that plan are planning on total control through their own white-washing monetary system and other dispositions.

You, however, need to make this a democratic system: a federation granting all nations representatives in two different segments, both from government and from the people.

Now of course you need to understand that those presently sitting in power stand to lose a huge amount of money. And they will not willingly see their own carefully structured plans go down the drain. But, there is no need to judge them, given their model of the world and their present thinking and understanding of the power they represent.

However, you are the people of the world and you by far out-number those few who are sitting in power at present. But you have not yet realised the power you have in your own truth, your own willingness to be honest and open, and that thereby you can require the truth from the others also.

Know that this is what will cause the breakdown of the current currency. Then the money will change colour and change value as you will start to value people for their effort, their energy spent by their labour, instead of qualifying their work by the education of the worker.

The first and foremost goal must be to secure for everyone in the world sufficient to cover their basic needs of food and shelter, and thereby give equal opportunities to all to move on in the world, sort of pursuing the 'American dream' as it was intended in the beginning.

Not everyone would want to pursue it much further than living from hand to mouth, but it is indeed their basic human right to be provided with their daily sustenance from you as a whole, being one great family. You are each other's caretakers when it comes to food and shelter.

From there on everybody must choose what he or she will do with their lives. Many will probably pursue their artistic abilities when presented with this possibility. But of course, there will still be enough other people who wish to make more money's worth out of their lives. And those who enjoy making money can produce work places and goods to be shared amongst you.

These people in business do of course have to have their incentives, but there must also be a limit on their possibilities for income, so that those who are going towards the top understand that this also gives them a responsibility; the responsibility to share their abundance. To give away the top tranches of their income as donations to charity in society.

Then you could all have a flat tax, for instance 10-15%, that everybody is requested to pay. Remember that there would be no more costs for military defence and only a small amount of health care, since the absence of fear would keep your inner defence system, the immune system, working as it was supposed to, lovingly attending to your own welfare....

This 'tax' would be the sort of tax that you willingly would pay for the good of all. Now, this is a grand vision of a future that you may choose when you are presented with this possibility.

And by the way, remember that you may have all the material comforts and things that please you – as long as you don't need any of them! You can have and enjoy them as long as the things don't start to own you – and they own you if you cannot do without them, can't afford to lose them or to share them with others...

Well, I need to go back to your own life and make you understand that all you are to sacrifice in this is just to stop hiding behind your illusions. Because the illusions are keeping you in ignorance, and when you reside in ignorance you cannot and will not do anything for the world. This is what makes you sit in your living room, passively watching your television as thousands and thousands of starving children pass by. But you do not do anything to help them because you feel it is not your personal problem.

Of course, as you think only in terms of what serves you, and you tend only to your own interests, you do not see the problem until you feel it could threaten your own safety and your investment in your own life's reality. But it is going to touch you at last, because you will no longer be able to close your eyes, once you have opened them...

Your heart will tell you that it is time to reconnect with the inner part of your being, and that inner part knows that you are part of the whole, that those starving children are indeed your responsibility, as a big brother or a wise sister. Because you need to give from your abundance, from your love, from your care and attention, so that they also can have what you take for granted.

It is indeed time for you to start realising that what happens to them is also influencing what is happening to you. As one humanity you cannot become happy until all those around you start to get their needs satisfied, because you are far and wide connected as one human race through each single human being.

Through the pages of its papers, through the news on television. the world media reminds you every day that you can no longer live happily with yourself by remaining in ignorance. And you will not have to for much longer either, because more and more is cracking up inside the corrupted systems that are ruling the world society at present.

So my responsibility to you is to open your eyes by opening your heart, to become part of your awareness and bring in the celestial news. And the present celestial news is indeed that I am continuing to live, yes, I am continuing to evolve and to learn.

I am indeed not silenced, although my body is buried 10 feet below in the ground. In other words, I may still do my duty to the people as a queen in your hearts...

Indeed I am soaring. My spirit is soaring as never before, and my voice is getting stronger and louder every day. So nobody can shut me up any more. And of course 'they' can not silence me any more, because they would not know how.

It would not help them in any way to try to remove my channel either, because then I would just find another voice, and then another, and then another. And then all of my conscious channels would come over here and continue our work through their celestial voices...

Besides, then you will also be my voice to the world – you will voice your own opinions, your own thoughts, and your own criticism of the system, the unfairness of the political situation as it is now. And you will continue my work, and I will continue, as we work together to better the constitution of the world.

We will soon be meeting again, after you have integrated what I have related to you in the three parts of this book. It needs to grow on you and open your consciousness towards your self and towards humanity. But when the pupil is ready, the teacher will come.

We are all in this together. You do your part and I will do mine. We will do this together, because together we are strong, we are united in oneness, and nobody can defeat oneness because it is all there is.

As you go to bed at night, call for your soul, call for your higher understanding, and ask your questions so as to receive the answer. And the next morning as you wake up, call again for the love from your soul. Call for your soul throughout the day and the result will be amazing. The result will be a new vision of a new life and a new way of conducting your affairs from the inside out. And you will start to plan for the day, not from the results of yesterday, but by looking into the future.

You will start to understand the grander perspective and take it into consideration when you plan for yourself; because it is not every man for himself, it is every man for everybody else. And so you will unite, and make for yourselves a proud Unified Federation of Nations. Nations that are independently ruling themselves through unity-thinking, with the motto, "The good for all is the good for the individual."

This is the way your soul will rule through your consciousness as you will find it in your heart to receive what you give, and give what you receive, out of love.

My love will be with you forever, for my love is your love, and our love is the love of The Creator for the creation that is who I am, and who you are. Thank you. You are all blessed, you are blessed with the blessing of your selves, as

I am

*Diana*

# Also from Findhorn Press . . .

# Books by Diana Cooper

Diana Cooper is a therapist, healer and author. Through her workshops and therapy she has helped countless people find their life mission, to fulfil their potential and empower their lives. During a crisis in her life she had a deep experience of an angelic being, which led her on an incredible inner journey into the Universe.

As a result of this she has devoted her life to healing, teaching and service, allowing the angels to support and guide her. She now constantly follows this inner guidance and lives what she believes.

---

"I believe in angels" is the title of a well-known song — but do we really?

With this book, we meet everyday folks who have experienced angels in their lives. Yes, angels do exist: they are highly evolved beings that have a lighter and faster vibration than humans, and are normally invisible to us. However, many of them have chosen to serve mankind and are available to help, support, heal and guide us — all we have to do is ask! There are small angels who care for the little daily tasks and enormous beings that overlight great universal projects. There are angels who can assist in healing and others who attend celebrations and rituals.

*A Little Light on Angels* gives us guidance on how we can call on them for help and companionship in our lives. We are surrounded by angels, all we have to do is raise our consciousness to become aware of them and communicate with them, to welcome them into our lives and allow the joy, light and peace of their presence into our hearts.

**A Little Light on Angels • ISBN 1-899171-51-7**

Do you want to live your life humming and glowing with joy?

Can you accept that ascension into light can be achieved this lifetime — and are you willing to do what it takes?

*A Little Light On Ascension* gives us all we need to fulfil our highest spiritual aspirations, thanks to easy-to-use techniques for purification, release, empowerment and ways of connecting with the Ascended Masters and Archangels.

Subjects covered include:

- Abundance
- Finding your mission
- Manifestation
- Inner peace
- Intergalactic work
- Spirit guides
- Ascension chambers
- Armageddon

Not for the faint-hearted, this book offers tools to anyone who wishes to accelerate their spiritual growth, enabling the reader to take advantage of the waves of ascension which are about to take place.

**A Little Light on Ascension • ISBN 1-899171-81-9**

---

Life can be a series of predicaments and challenges. However, if we choose to, we can learn something even from the darkest moments. Life presents us with a multitude of difficult questions, but if we listen to that still inner voice inside us, we will surely find inspiring and uplifting answers, which will bring us joy and peace. In a sometimes harsh world, *Golden Footsteps* is a treasure of hope and joy.

**Golden Footsteps • ISBN 1-899171-71-1**

# Books by Marko Pogačnik

Slovenian artist Marko Pogacnik has acquired an international reputation in conceptual and land art. He leads seminars in earth healing in several countries and provides advice on landscape matters for communities and businesses. Marko is a lecturer at the Hagia Chora School.

This book is remarkable in that almost everything described in the book is based on the author's own practical experiences in communicating with these beings through meditation and tuning into plants, trees, animals and the landscape. He describes in detail the various elemental beings and their roles in maintaining the web of life, and also gives insights into related topics, such as the flow of energies within landscape, and the long-suppressed Goddess culture. His evocative images of the nature spirits draw our attention to the lost harmony of the natural world which has been disrupted by the impact of human culture.

• "This is a remarkable book by one of Europe's most important spiritual teachers. It provides unique and entertaining insights into the world of earth spirits and fairy folk. This is important information for the imagination and for healing the earth." — William Bloom

**Nature Spirits & Elemental Beings:**
**Working with the Intelligence in Nature**
**• ISBN 1-899171-66-5**

Thanks to the global ecological movement, people everywhere have begun to realize the destructive consequences of our civilization's uncontrolled development. This book takes the next step and directs public awareness to the destructive processes that, almost unnoticed, endanger the invisible subtle systems of nature, the landscape and life on earth. What actually happens to the earth when one of its heart chakras is ruthlessly blocked by a building that has been erected without sensitivity? When a wall with a 'no-man's-land' cuts an integral landscape into two (the Berlin Wall, which still stands despite having been physically dismantled)? When massive constructions of steel and concrete slice through the sensitive energy lines of the earth (road networks)? All this leads to blockages and imbalances in the subtle organs and energy systems of the earth which culminate in a life-endangering malfunction.

**Healing the Heart of the Earth:**
**Restoring the Subtle Levels of Life**
**• ISBN 1-899171-57-6**

---

This book tells of Pogacnik's discovery of a fifth gospel hidden in the sub-texts of the four other gospels. It teaches humanity how to live in the third millennium. He has translated around 100 saying of Jesus into a language that modern mind can understand, and identifies blockages in the four gospels that have prevented the Spirit of Christ to manifest fully in the past era. We are offered, this once only, the opportunity of overcoming the ancient division between heaven and earth, spirit and matter. In the process of human evolution and consciousness, heaven and earth will be united. Jesus points to this goal. In his gospels is buried a message which mankind is now ready to hear. To decipher this message, Pogacnik has used various methods and had the help of the angelic and elemental realms. The drawings found in the book are presented not just for the reader's information, but to energize him or her with the power of life and impart an instinctive synergy with the thought-flow of the book.

**Living Earth and the Presence of Christ: A Fifth Gospel**
**• ISBN 1-899171-92-4  (autumn 1999)**

# FINDHORN Press

Findhorn Press is the publishing business of the Findhorn Community which has grown around the Findhorn Foundation in northern Scotland.

For further information about the Findhorn Foundation and the Findhorn Community, please contact:

## Findhorn Foundation

The Visitors Centre
The Park, Findhorn IV36 3TY, Scotland, UK
tel 01309 690311• fax 01309 691301
email reception@findhorn.org
www.findhorn.org

For a complete Findhorn Press catalogue, please contact:

## Findhorn Press

The Park, Findhorn,
Forres IV36 3TY
Scotland, UK
Tel 01309 690582

Fax 01309 690036

P. O. Box 13939
Tallahassee
Florida 32317-3939, USA
Tel (850) 893 2920
toll-free 1-877-390-4425
Fax (850) 893 3442

e-mail info@findhornpress.com
http://www.findhornpress.com